GOOD
MANNERS
for Today's Kids

Bob & Emilie Barnes

HARVEST HOUSE PUBLISHERS
EUGENE, OREGON

Cover by e210 Design, Eagan, Minnesota

Cover photo © Veer Marketplace / Veer

Portions of this book include modified excerpts from the following titles:

 A Little Book of Manners © 1998 by Emilie Barnes (with Anne Christian Buchanan)
 A Little Book of Manners for Boys © 2000 by Bob and Emilie Barnes
 Good Manners for Every Occasion © 2008 by Emilie Barnes

GOOD MANNERS FOR TODAY'S KIDS
Copyright © 2010 by Bob and Emilie Barnes
Published by Harvest House Publishers
Eugene, Oregon 97402
www.harvesthousepublishers.com

Library of Congress Cataloging-in-Publication Data
 Barnes, Bob, 1933-
 Good manners for today's kids / Bob and Emilie Barnes.
  p. cm.
 ISBN 978-0-7369-2811-3 (pbk.)
 1. Etiquette for children and teenagers. I. Barnes, Emilie. II. Title.
 BJ1857.C5B346 2009
 395.1'22—dc22
                 2009017188

Printed in the United States of America

    10 11 12 13 14 15 16 17 18 / VP-NI / 10 9 8 7 6 5 4 3 2 1

*Children are the sum of what parents
contribute to their lives.*

RICHARD R. STRAUSS

～～

This book is dedicated to you because you want
your children to have good manners and become
adults who practice kindness and courtesy.

It takes a lot of time and commitment to teach
social graces. May God continue to give you the
added strength and energy to teach manners
through your actions, words, these lessons, and
the way your family treats one another. Every day
presents an opportunity to grow and show manners.

As you instill and follow good manners, you will
receive the blessing of a happier home and kinder,
more compassionate children.

Contents

Section Four: The Delight of Dining Etiquette

Section Five: The Comfort of Confidence at All Times

Section Six: The Gift of Friendships and Relationships

The Lifetime Legacy of Manners

Manners are the happy ways of doing things.

RALPH WALDO EMERSON

When people talk about teaching manners to today's kids, they are often referring to infusing their children's vocabulary with "please" and "thank you." Courteous language is wonderful and presents an initial impression of manners, but there is so much more that you can pass along to your children to improve their lives, their futures as confident adults, and the daily life of your family today. The legacy of manners that you begin creating now will greatly enhance the life of your child from this point onward.

The challenge is set before you. Our young ones, preteens, and teens make up a generation of "finger eaters" that is more familiar with (and inclined to want) drive-through windows than dining tables. They grow up interacting with adults and peers using a very casual attitude and, therefore, are less likely to develop a sense of respect for, and collaboration with, authority. Immediate access to information and to people via the wonders of technology can circumvent any perceived need for a more mannerly approach to communication.

Not many of us would want to give up the technology that is at our fingertips. In fact many of us thrive in the fast-paced climate. But it doesn't take much soul-searching to realize that remarkable technological advancements and the "on the go" lifestyle that result from those advancements are both blessings *and* burdens. Excellent manners and considerate, social behaviors actually make today's culture more of a blessing and less of a burden; we just have to put those manners into practice personally and in the life-lesson curriculum we're teaching our children.

We juggle many responsibilities as well as many distractions. One hectic or overly planned day follows on the heels of another, and soon it is hard to look past ourselves to what others need. We ask, "What's in it for me?" because we are just getting by. And our kids are saying, "What's in it for me?" because they are watching us. To have proper graces, we need to set our minds toward a new direction and horizon—one that encompasses us and others. Our children will notice this emphasis on helping, serving, and loving one another. They will feel the security of it in their own homes and will be more inclined to emulate it no matter where they go and how fast they grow.

Compared to earlier decades, the current climate in the home and workplace is far more casual. In fact, many of today's parents have not grown up with a foundation of instruction in the area of manners. Because of this lack of understanding and a loss of our society's encouragement of manners, parents must have a sincere desire for their children to have a stronger foundation in manners than they had. This will take a concerted effort, but it is energy and commitment that is well worth it! The dividends last for generations. We're so glad that you've decided to pursue nurturing your child's character through teaching good manners.

The Golden Rule is found in the Bible: "Treat others as you want them to treat you" (Luke 6:31 TLB). This is the core value of good manners and good etiquette. It requires that we have an understanding of other people and their needs. It is also an important bit of wisdom that helps all of us get along at home and in social circles.

Social graces are positive rules, guidelines, and cues that make it easier to interact with people and live a day-by-day pleasant life. If you know how to dine with others and how to introduce and meet others, you'll be more at ease and comfortable in your social interactions and with family members. Manners smooth out the rough edges of life. They civilize us. Treating people of all ages and walks of life properly is the right thing to do. Being kind, thoughtful, and considerate will never go out of style, and it will suit every occasion, every time.

Good manners start with following basic rules and priorities, and bad manners start with disregarding the basic rules and priorities. What could be simpler? So why are so many people in our society lacking basic social skills? The answer is simple: we have a lack of knowledge, training, encouragement, and examples. And when social skills fall into disuse, we return to survival skills that barely get us through the day. Good manners for kids start at home. The Hebrew word for parent translates to "teacher." That means you both, Mom and Dad; you have the responsibility to teach your children proper manners and courtesies. And it's easier if you start when they are young. It's not done all at once but little by little and precept by precept.

One of the most influential ways you'll teach a child is by your actions in your home. If the Golden Rule is important to you, it will be meaningful to your children. If it is a genuine part of your lifestyle, heart, and character, it will become a part of the legacy you leave them.

Interactive Manners Moments

At the start of each of the sections in this book, we speak directly to you, the parent. We want to give you a foundation for the topic that is to be studied in the pages that follow. After we've talked to you, the actual manners moments and tips are almost all in sections written to your children from the perspective of another child. These "Kid-2-Kid" sections stand out as important portions of the book.

How you use the Kid-2-Kid sections is up to you and your family. If your children are little, you can read these fun sections out loud to them as part of your manners school or family time. If your kids are in grade school or older, have them read these sections out loud to you. If you have several children, have them take turns. Mom and Dad can also be a part of the reading rotation. This keeps the whole family involved, and it helps build (you guessed it) manners! Reading aloud will create a foundation of confidence for your children. And the entire family will learn the skills of speaking and listening to show respect for others.

Be sure to stop and discuss each section, no matter how brief it is, so that the information sinks in. New readers might not retain as much information as the older kids when they read aloud. And discussing each manners lesson keeps this book personal for all of you.

Some portions are from a girl's perspective (Emilie Marie)

and some are from a boy's perspective. As you and your children explore manners, help them apply the manners lesson to situations they have been in or ones they might face in the future. The gender perspectives will add dimension and more examples to discuss, but don't let them get in the way of teaching the universal lesson being explored in each section.

Help for Every Occasion

Our hope has been to provide a well-rounded gathering of illustrations and lessons. Some lessons, we focus on different angles, such as hosting guests and being a guest, serving dinner to others and being served. It is helpful for children to understand how manners apply at home and in every home they enter.

A good way to make the most of the many suggestions is to list the categories of manners your child, or your family as a whole, needs to work on. This makes it fun to single out those areas that could use a bit of "extra attention" instead of being called embarrassing or bad behaviors. After all, we are still learning these skills as adults. We certainly don't expect a five-year-old or nine-year-old to have these down. Not yet anyway!

❦

Enjoy the journey. It can be fun, and you certainly will enjoy the final product: children you can be proud of and children who are comfortable expressing themselves, their ideas, and their compassion for others.

May this book be a source of encouragement and guidance as you delight in the rich, generous, and abundant life that comes from embracing the best behaviors for everyday living.

*The hardest job kids face today is
learning good manners without seeing any.*

Fred Astaire

Manners School in Session

Weekends, family nights, or the summer vacation months are a great time to conduct a manners school with your children. You can use the six sections in this book as your manners school format, or you can evaluate how to break down the sections into smaller portions and create your own lesson plans. No matter how you decide to use this book, the times you and your child spend learning together will be very special and lasting.

A Good Starting Place

Ultimately, manners are about taking responsibility for one's own actions, words, behaviors, and attitudes. There isn't an area of our lives that isn't improved when good manners are demonstrated. Before you start officially going through the book, it might be good to introduce the idea of manners lessons over dinner one evening. Or even better...make popcorn, invite the family to the living room or the back porch, and have an open discussion about manners. Topics that might be discussed as a family are:

- Why it is important to develop good manners
- How to notice and encourage good manners when used by family members

- Why taking responsibility at home is a part of the well-mannered life
- How to follow through with basic chores
- Basic skills in assigned areas of responsibility
- How the equipment in the kitchen works
- How to have polite and interesting conversations at meals
- Why treating people with respect is important and godly
- When to speak up and when to be silent

There are so many areas that call for personal responsibility and appropriate behavior. That's why you've picked up this book! Personalize your manners school for your family's situation as you follow through on the topics in each section of this book.

There is no place in the world where
courtesy is so necessary as in the home.

HELEN HATHAWAY

The Right Moves of Respect

Respect Is at the Heart of Manners

Manners are the sincere, considerate, and simple
expressions of important values in everyday life.
PEGGY POST

It doesn't take long to spot people with good manners. They are the people others enjoy being around. As parents, you can point out the people in your family's world who have great manners so that your kids will understand what makes those persons special and why. And, of course, you'll be their primary role models!

Well-mannered persons always have an abundance of friends and make friends easily at social gatherings because they genuinely care about the people they meet. They express sincere warmth in their greetings and put others at ease. The kindness they exhibit on the outside reflects their commitment to the Golden Rule on the inside. In some fashion they share the following characteristics and values:

- *Tact*—Mannerly persons value honesty and also realize they needn't be brutally frank when talking with others. Speaking one's mind is not always a virtue. One must learn to sometimes set aside ones personal opinions and biases. And one must always think before one acts or speaks. Remember, you never have to apologize for words you haven't spoken. Tactful persons know how easily thoughtless words or deeds can hurt others, so they guard their tongues.

- *Self-confidence*—Have you been around very confident people? They seem to inspire confidence in others because they aren't worried about their every move and comment and decision. They are very positive and often direct in their approach to life. You seldom hear them concentrate on the negative aspects of life, and therefore those around them do the same. Confidence is infectious.

- *Flexibility*—A mannerly person understands that etiquette is an expression of cultural and social values. We would expect that someone from one country might do things one way and a person from another country, a different way. One must learn to modify or change one's etiquette and manners to accommodate the traditions of other countries and cultures. This doesn't mean you stop being on your best behavior; it just means you observe the culture you are in and respect its standards before you act or speak.

- *Common sense*—One would think that common sense would be common, but that doesn't seem to be the case anymore. Persons with good manners know how to facilitate good relationships by adapting to the needs of others without sacrificing their own values. These persons know how to choose their battles while also understanding that not all battles are worth the fight.

Good manners don't limit anyone's ability to act boldly or think deeply; instead, they permit people to disagree agreeably.

- *Respect*—We live in a world that is very diverse, and we are to respect others' rights and opinions. If we disagree with a point being made, we can wait and discuss our differences in private. A well-mannered person needs to respect differing points of view. We are to treat others as we would have others treat us.

A person who reflects the above traits can function very well in all kinds of situations and settings. These traits are most important in everyday relationships and within families, where respectful and considerate behavior cements the bond of love and affection.

The last value and trait, *respect,* is what we will address in this section. There is an undercurrent of disrespect among members of the younger generation. They are losing sight of what it means to respect their elders and the wisdom their elders offer. They lean toward a "me first" attitude and therefore devalue others, including their peers and siblings. As they watch adults casually dispose of, replace, or upgrade objects, the importance of maintaining and caring for their possessions becomes a less important concept. Perhaps the most dangerous force of this undercurrent of disrespect is the lack of respect for themselves. When a child loses or never claims a sense of self-respect, he or she certainly cannot see the value of respecting anyone or anything else.

By teaching your children what respect looks and feels like, and where it comes from, you will give them tools to lead, follow, listen, serve, communicate, persevere, share their faith, and stand firm for their principles. Don't we all need to be reminded that we are valued and loved and that we are special children of God?

This truth is where respect comes from and flows out of. What a wonderful conversation you can have with your children about this vital value!

Thankfully, good manners can be learned at any age, but when the learning process begins in childhood, mannerly behavior becomes more natural. Parents, that's why it's so important to begin teaching good manners when your children are young. It's always easier to prevent bad habits from being formed than to try correcting bad behaviors that have already become habits. An early start takes advantage of a child's instinct to learn.

Manners School Family Activity: Etiquette Quiz

All the categories for manners are important, but one way to focus on your trouble areas is to take the following quiz. If you have older kids, you can have them take this quiz independently, and then you can each share your score. If you have younger kids or want to make this the kick-off activity for your manners school, do this quiz together. It's fun, and it will shed light on the missing manners in your family members' lives! Take time to discuss the quiz. There are some obvious answers and a few that might stump your child. Talk about how good manners and bad manners impact everyone, every day.

Etiquette IQ Test

These "yes" or "no" questions will help you know where your strengths are and where you need the most focused attention. Write your answers on a separate sheet of paper. When your family finishes taking the quiz together or separately, you can read the answers aloud. You might be surprised by a few of the responses!

1. If you aren't sure which utensil to use at a social gathering, it is best to watch the host or hostess and follow the leader.

   Yes   No

2. It's okay to talk loudly on your cell phone or to someone at a different table when you are in a restaurant.

   Yes   No

3. Before you bring a friend or extra family member to a gathering or a dinner, you should check with the host.

   Yes   No

4. It's proper to blow bubbles in your drink with a straw at a restaurant.

   Yes   No

5. When setting the table, you place the salad fork to the left of the dinner fork.

   Yes   No

6. It's okay to reach for a basket of bread if you don't knock over someone's glass of water.

   Yes   No

7. If you need to use a toothpick to dislodge a bit of food from between your teeth, you should excuse yourself and go to the restroom.

   Yes   No

8. When you receive a gift, it isn't necessary to send a thank-you note.

   Yes   No

9. It's okay to butter all of your bread at one time— thus saving your energy.

   Yes   No

10. The dinner knife should be placed to the right of your plate with the sharp edge facing out.

    Yes   No

11. When passing food at the dining table, you pass to the left.

    Yes   No

12. It is okay to send a thank-you note by e-mail or text message.

    Yes   No

13. When sending out invitations to a social event, you need to allow adequate time for the guests to respond.

    Yes   No

14. When leaving the table during the meal, you should place your napkin to the right of your plate.

    Yes   No

15. Your cell phone should be turned off when you are at church.

    Yes   No

16. It's okay to go to a funeral, church, or wedding in casual attire.

    Yes   No

17. You need to call the host of a party if you become sick earlier in the day and know you will not attend that evening's event.

    Yes   No

18. It's proper for a young man to extend certain courtesies to a young lady.

    Yes   No

19. A gentleman should not offer to shake hands with a lady until she first offers her hand to shake.

    Yes   No

20. The signal to tell your waiter that you are finished with your meal is to place your knife and fork at the nine o'clock position on your plate.

    Yes   No

Proper answers

1. Yes; 2. No; 3. Yes; 4. No; 5. Yes; 6. No; 7. Yes; 8. No; 9. No; 10. No; 11. No; 12. No; 13. Yes; 14. No; 15. Yes; 16. No; 17. Yes; 18. Yes; 19. Yes; 20. No

Score card—count up the number of correct answers

0–5: You really need this book. URGENT!

6–10: You need a refresher course or a beginner's class.

11–15: You're on the right track, but more is to be learned.

16–18: Your parents did a good job training you.

19–20: Go to the head of the class.

Be a Good Sport: Respecting Others

Do you like team sports like basketball and soccer? Or do you prefer the "extreme" stuff—skateboarding, snowboarding, mountain biking? Or do you like chess or computer games best of all? Sports and games can be a lot of fun, but they can also end in everyone's getting upset if something goes wrong. That's why you need to remember your manners when you play, whether competitively or for fun. These are things that guys and girls of all ages need to practice.

Know the Rules

Have you ever played a game with someone who made up the rules as he went along—and those rules always helped *him* to win? That's not any fun. It's also not fun to play with kids who have no clue how a game should be played—and don't want to learn. When you're on a team or in a P.E. class, listen up when your coach or teacher explains the rules. By learning them, you won't have to think so much while you're playing about what to do, and it will be easier to get the hang of things. If you're just playing a game at recess or at a friend's house, follow along and learn the rules as much as you can. If you're not sure about something, you can always ask someone to explain it.

Winning and Losing

Sure, it's fun to win, but the old saying is true—you're a winner or a loser based on your attitude. When you win, thank your opponent for the good game. You can say something like, "Nice passing," or "Great hustle." When you lose, do the same thing! Shake hands or give high-fives. Smile and tell your opponent that you'll be ready next time—and you probably will be!

It is never acceptable to boo the other team or the officials who are enforcing the rules on the field of play. You always want to be courteous even if they make a wrong call.

Playing Fair

Cheaters don't end up playing for very long. Whether it's lying about how many points you have in a game of one-on-one or peeking at the answers during a trivia game, nobody wants to play with a cheater. It takes all the fun out of the game. So admit that you fouled Fred, and let him shoot his free throws. Tell Tommy that his tennis serve was in, even if he thinks it might have gone out. Don't restart the computer game when Chad goes out of the room for a drink of water. Never trash talk. If you make a mistake or your team loses, don't make excuses. Just say, "My fault," and work extra hard the next time.

Most of the time the people you play games with are your friends. And when you're playing on a team, your teammates and opponents are usually pretty good sports. But every now and then you'll run into someone who's truly a bad sport—a kid who plays dirty, hogs the ball, or says mean things to you. Many games are lost because you or a team member breaks a rule. It's always best to play fair and abide by the rules. If the bad sport is on your team, you and a few of the other kids can try talking to him. If that doesn't seem to help, talk to the coach. If the poor sport is on the other team, ignore him if you can. If things get bad, call a timeout and have your team captain talk to the ref. And if things get *super* bad and a fight breaks out during the game, walk away and let the grown-ups handle it. And—this should be obvious—don't *you* be the one starting anything.

Hurt Player

You're playing basketball, the score is tied, and suddenly the other team's star player goes down with a bad knee injury. He's already scored four goals, and with him out of the game, your team has a really good shot at winning. So what do you do? Celebrate the fact that he's hurt? Taunt the other team? Neither. What you should do is show your support for him. Clap with everyone else once he gets up and makes his way off the court. If he's around after the game, stop by and tell him how well he played. Tell him you hope his knee is better soon.

Being a Fan

Manners don't just apply to the people playing the game. Fans need to have good manners too! It's okay to get really excited about an event or a favorite player, but it's never okay to yell rude things, swear, boo loudly, or throw food or other objects. You *can* get really into cheering for your team. (Just don't make the people around you deaf!) If the person behind you asks you to sit down, have a seat. There will be plenty of time to stand up and cheer the good plays. It's fun to go crazy at a sporting event, and you may as long as you remember your manners for being a fantastic fan.

When we're playing games, good manners means being good sports—not cheating, not using mean language, not bragging when we win or pouting when we lose. Everybody wins sometimes and loses sometimes. What's important is for all of us to do our best, encourage one another, and have fun—whether we're playing soccer, Monopoly, or tic-tac-toe.

Visiting and Welcoming Friends: Respecting the Home

I really have fun with my friends from school, church, and my neighborhood. But I never thought about being *polite* to these friends—until Aunt Jenny mentioned it. She said that manners help me get along a lot better anywhere I work and play—even with my friends.

Aunt Jenny said, "Love has manners." Well, friendship has manners too. The very best way to show good manners with my friends is to be a friend.

A Real Friend

Being a friend means being loyal and honest. It means keeping secrets and promises, helping each other out, and thinking about each other's feelings. It means being a good listener. And, of course, being a friend means having fun and doing things together.

But being a friend *doesn't* mean whispering or telling secrets in front of someone else. It doesn't mean ganging up on someone or leaving someone out or making fun of someone who is not in the group.

Saying bad things or lying about other people is always bad manners—even when I'm mad. I can really hurt other people by telling stories about them. Even telling true stories—to a parent, teacher, or someone my age—can be impolite if I use those stories just to get my own way or make someone else look bad.

Being a polite person means treating everybody with everyday good manners, even unpopular people or people who act strange or weird. I don't have to be everyone's best friend. But I should try to treat everyone I meet with kindness and respect. That means not making fun of people and never laughing at them.

Making a Friend Welcome at My House

One of my favorite things to do with my friends is go over to each other's houses. Sometimes we go over to play for the afternoon. Sometimes we get together to do homework or to work on a project. Sometimes we have sleepovers, which are really fun.

No matter how long the visit, having a friend over to my house requires a special set of good manners. Aunt Jenny calls this kind of manners "hospitality." It means making my guests feel welcome and special and helping them have a good time at my house.

Hospitality manners start with meeting my guests at the door or even in front of the house and saying, "Hi, come on in."

I show them where they can put their coats and things, and I show them where the kitchen and bathrooms are. I introduce them to my family if they don't already know them, and I tell them about any house rules they need to know.

After that, it's always polite to offer my guests something to eat or drink. Even if I don't have any juice or raisins or my mom doesn't want me to have a snack right then, I should at least offer my friend a drink of water.

Showing hospitality to my guests also means putting them first while they're over at my house. I offer them the biggest cookie, the best chair, and (if they're staying overnight) the most comfortable bed. And I try to do what they want to do (most of the time).

I don't say:

"This is my house, so we're going to do what I want."

Instead, I say,

"You're the guest. What do you want to do?"

One special part of hospitality means sharing my things with a visitor. If she wants to play with my toy horses or my dolls, I should let her. If there is something special I don't want her playing with, I should ask my mom to help me put it away before my guest arrives.

If my guest is staying overnight or even longer, there are a few more things I can do for her. If she forgot her pajamas, I can lend her some of mine. (My mom also keeps extra toothbrushes and stuff in case visitors forget theirs.) I make sure she has a comfy pillow to sleep on, and I ask her if she needs a nightlight. I ask her what she likes for breakfast. And I do whatever I can to help her feel right at home. That's really what hospitality—and good host manners—means.

Being the Guest

If I'm visiting at someone else's house, my manners job is a little different. My job is to fit in to my friend's household and make it easy for her family to have me as a guest. It's also important to show that I appreciate her hospitality.

One thing that is very nice to do when I visit someone's house is to bring a little gift for the family. This kind of gift is called a "hostess gift." This isn't necessary if I just go over to Barbara's house for the afternoon, but it's a nice thing to do if I'm invited to dinner or to spend the night. A hostess gift doesn't have to be fancy or expensive. It can be a candle or a little plant or some cookies I baked or some flowers I picked from my garden. My mom or Aunt Jenny always helps me choose a nice gift to bring when I go to visit.

Whether I bring a gift or not, I always owe my hosts the gift of my respect and thanks. It is nice of them to let me come over. I should tell them so, and I should also show my respect by the way I act.

Remembering to wipe my feet at the door is a part of showing respect for my hosts. So is hanging up my coat and keeping my other belongings out of the way. I show respect by keeping my feet off the furniture and my hands off ornaments and decorations. I don't turn on the TV, the radio, or the DVD player unless I'm invited to. And I help clean up any mess we make while we are playing.

It's also important to respect the privacy of my host and her family. Even though they are sharing their house with me, that doesn't give me the right to open drawers, peek in closets, or read private papers, no matter how curious I am. I certainly shouldn't use their things or try on their clothes without being invited to!

What should you do if you need something? There's nothing wrong with asking for a tissue or a drink of water, but you shouldn't demand things like snacks or treats. Instead, you should wait for your hosts to offer something. If what they offer is not your favorite, you shouldn't say so or ask for something else. You should just say thank you and enjoy the company of your friend.

If you're invited for a meal, all your best mealtime manners apply. You should try to have a nice conversation with your friend and her family. You should also offer to help with setting the table, preparing the meal, or cleaning up.

One thing you should never say as a guest is "At my house

we…" That sounds like your hosts' house isn't good enough, and it makes them feel bad. Besides, you're not at your house! You're in their house, and that means you follow their house rules—for bedtime, chores, and anything else.

If you're staying overnight or for several days, it's even more important to try to fit in with the way the household works. You should pick up after yourself and not leave your things lying around. It's easy to get casual in the bathroom, but be sure to fold your towel neatly and hang it up, and put the lids back on toothpaste and shampoo containers. Take the extra step and help your friend clean up her room too. And always knock before opening a closed door.

And you should both try to keep the noise level down, even if you're giggling in your room late at night. Sometimes it is hard to get to sleep when you're having a sleepover…but you shouldn't keep the other people in the house up all night.

When it's time to leave, you shouldn't wear out your welcome by hanging around. Most important of all, you need to say a big thank you to your friend and her family.

"Thanks for having me. I'm glad I came!"

"And I'm really glad that you're my friend."

The heart of visiting manners is to be a thoughtful host and a thankful guest. A good guest doesn't complain or demand, doesn't snoop, follows house rules, picks up after herself, and always says thank you!

And when you get home, don't forget to write a thank-you note to your host.

There are good ships, and there are bad ships,
but the best ships are friendships.

Stuff, Privacy, and Public Places: Respecting People's Things

We've all been taught that it's people who matter, not things. But people *have* things. So to treat people right, we have to treat their things right too. And the same good manners apply no matter where we are—in our own houses, at a friend's or relative's home, on a camping trip, or even at the local swimming pool.

In Your Own House

Your room might be neat as a pin—but if you're like most kids, it probably isn't! Try to keep it as clean as you can, especially when company is coming over or your parents ask you to pick it up. And try to keep the other rooms of the house cleaner than your room. When you work on your science project in the basement or garage, be sure to clean up after yourself—or you might end up with an even bigger project on your hands! Remember to keep the outside pretty tidy too, and put away your skateboard, basketball, or other toys when you're done with them. Besides keeping things neat, this also prevents your stuff from getting lost, stolen, or broken by your little brother.

At Someone Else's Home

It's tempting to snoop around someone else's house, but people close doors and drawers for a reason. They'd leave them wide open if they wanted you to see what was inside! The same goes for private talks. It's definitely *not* good manners to exercise your spy skills here. Do your best to follow the schedule of the people you're visiting—go to bed when they do, get up when they do, eat meals and snacks when you're supposed to. You'll definitely be invited back if you practice your word manners like *please* and *thank you*. And even if that package of Oreos on the shelf is calling out your name, wait until you're offered before you eat any.

Speaking of eating, be brave when trying new foods, especially foods from other countries. Many Americans don't know what they're missing until they try Japanese, Thai, or Greek food. And here's a really important manner to remember: Don't comment out loud on the "weird" way other people do things. Instead, thank them for having you over.

It's also nice to bring your friend's mom something called a "hostess gift." It doesn't have to be fancy or cost a lot. It can even be a flower picked from your garden. Remember to put your manners in your pocket and take them with you!

In the Great Outdoors

Treat the outdoors with just as much respect as you would treat anything indoors. The outdoors belong to everyone! When you're out hiking or snowboarding in the mountains or camping or fishing by a lake, pick up your trash and leave plants and animals where you found them, no matter how cool that snake would look in your room or how much your mom would like that flowering bush. A good rule of thumb is to leave any place cleaner than you found it—even in the middle of the woods.

Other People's Belongings

Lots of times kids your age earn a little bit of money taking care of pets and houses or apartments when a friend or neighbor goes on a trip. You might be in charge of feeding the cats, picking up the mail and paper, and making sure everything looks okay. The family will probably leave you a list of things to do. Make sure you read *and* follow the list—exactly! Give Fluffy her liver and gristle cat food, even if you think she'd like your family's leftover salmon loaf much better. Leave the mail unopened, even if you really want to read that letter from the principal to B.J.'s parents. If you do a great job, chances are you'll be asked to look after things again.

Accidents Happen

Even when we are very careful, accidents happen. It's always best to be honest when those situations occur. Suppose you break an art object that may not seem too valuable to you, but the owner has had it in the family for fifty years—what do you do? The main thing is to be honest. Tell the owner right away what happened. Don't try to hide the broken pieces or blame someone else. While you won't be able to replace the broken item, you can make things a little better by writing an "I'm sorry" note. Giving a bouquet of flowers can give a big lift to the person too.

If you accidentally break something like a window or a dish and tell the truth about it right away, your parents will probably help you replace the item. It helps to remember that accidents happen to everyone and that most people are quick to forgive.

▶ Kid-2-Kid ◀

Soap, Showers, and Socks:
Respecting Your Self

Have you combed your hair today? Do your socks match, and are they clean? Did you hang up your towel after your shower or bath? (Did you *take* a shower or bath?) When did you last brush your teeth? Floss them? Yep, you're probably ready for a crash course in personal manners—or *hygiene*. And even if you're doing a pretty good job in this department, everyone needs a little reminder from time to time. Of course you get muddy or sweaty when you're playing soccer or wear old, torn clothes when you're mountain biking or skateboarding. But certain situations call for nicer clothing, and it's always good to be *somewhat* clean.

Even though girls don't usually do all the heavy sweaty types of activities, they need to go by the same hygiene rules as boys. Doing so will make everyone just smell better.

The Basics

If you want your friends to keep hanging around you and you don't want your parents to move your living quarters out to the garage, it's important to keep a few basics in mind. Take a bath or shower every day, if you can. Wash your face then too. Brush your teeth after each meal, and try to remember to floss, especially if you wear braces. Wash your hands—a lot! Don't dig dirty clothes out of the hamper, even if they are your favorites. You can wear something else that's clean, wait till the laundry is done, or—better yet—learn to do your own laundry.

Because girls usually have longer hair than boys, they will spend more time caring for their hair. For good hygiene, wash your hair with shampoo as needed. Each girl's hair is unique to her. One girl's hair needs more care than the next girl's. Even sisters have different care requirements. Healthy-looking hair is a sign of good hair hygiene.

The Right Stuff

Would you snowboard in a tuxedo? Go swimming in a fleece coat? Climb Mount Everest in your swim trunks? It's important to wear the right stuff for the right situation, isn't it? So remember that the next time Mom begs you to please, *please,* please put on something else to visit Aunt Donna. While it's true that visiting your aunt isn't a sport, it's also true that the visit will probably go better if everyone's okay with how everyone else looks. So dress a little nicer for things like school, church, going out to eat, and going to other people's houses. Don't make a big deal if your parents ask you to change into something different. They're probably not asking you to wear anything really ridiculous, like a three-piece suit and a top hat. You'll have plenty of chances to wear your old jeans and faded T-shirts.

The way you dress shows the respect you have for the occasion. You only get one chance to make the right impression. Always put your best foot forward. It's always better to be overdressed than underdressed.

Splish, Splash

When you're taking care of personal stuff, be sure to also practice good bathroom manners. Put the toilet seat down when you're done with it. Mop up any puddles of water on the floor or countertop. Hang up your towel to dry. Clean any dirt and toothpaste out of the sink and off of the counters. Wipe down the mirrors, and turn on the fan if the room is really steamy. And save some hot water for other family members who still need to shower. Those icy showers are the worst!

Girls, if you have to share a bathroom with your brothers or other members of the family, remember not to take too long in the bathroom. They, too, have to use the bathroom.

How Not to Get Sick

Sneeze! Sniffle! Cough! It's cold season…and flu season…and whatever-other-bug-is-floating-around-out-there season. Did you know that good manners can help keep you from getting sick? It's true! So here's what you do. Wash your hands *a lot.* That helps stop the spread of germs that cause colds, flu, and all that other icky junk. Always wash your hands after you go to the bathroom or before you eat something. If you do get sick, it's good manners to stay home and not pass your germs on to everyone else. Blow your nose into a tissue. Never wipe it with your sleeve or with the back of your hand. Staying clean helps you stay healthy.

Guys, remember that your shirt sleeve is not a Kleenex. Carry extra tissues and/or a handkerchief in your back pocket when you have a runny nose.

Dressing Your Best

Lots of schools these days have uniforms, even public schools. And if the students at your school don't wear uniforms, chances are they do have to follow a dress code. Why do schools make kids dress a certain way? And what can you do if you really can't stand the uniform or dress code? First off, keep in mind that right now, going to school is your job. Lots and lots of grown-ups wear uniforms for their jobs—surgeons wear scrubs, professional basketball players wear shorts, jerseys, and high tops, and police officers wear a full uniform that even includes a car or motorcycle!

Your school uniform might not include a motorcycle, but it probably looks a lot like regular school clothes and is also pretty comfortable, right? It sure makes getting dressed in the morning easy. You can wear the other things in your closet after school and on the weekends, except for tomorrow when you have a soccer game. Guess what you'll put on then? That's right—a uniform! It's good to learn at an early age to be respectful of authority.

*The greatest thing a man can do for his heavenly Father
is to be kind to some of His other children.*

Henry Drummond

The Enjoyment of Effective Communication

Everyday Kindnesses in Action

Out of the overflow of the heart the mouth speaks.
The good man brings good things out
of the good stored up in him.

MATTHEW 12:34-35

Some kinds of manners are for special situations and special occasions, but most manners are good for any time and every occasion. How we engage in daily conversation with others is a key part of how we extend a heart of good manners and put everyday kindnesses into action. Sometimes we and our children are on our best behavior while in public settings, but then we forget to be gracious and generous to one another when we are at home. We get tired. We get bothered by the habits of one another. We get lazy. But the home front is where we perfect the language of love and kindness. When members of the family know they are loved—because they receive confirmation of that wonderful fact through daily words and actions in the home—they will more easily share from a gentle heart with neighbors, friends, strangers, and other family members.

You are creating a lasting, influential legacy when you speak with love toward your spouse, your children, and others. Please don't forget others! If you criticize coworkers, a friend, or your spouse, the little ears near you will hear it and take it to heart. When you make a joke about another person or speak with sarcasm, your children won't view the comments as humorous; they will recognize them as hurtful. We should all have the sensitivity of children! Then we would speak with much more compassion, and we would love without condition or judgment.

Maybe today you can begin to think and speak with a child's heart. It will change the tone of your home in a matter of days. This section is an important one to go through with your child. As he or she reads aloud or listens to the Kid-2-Kid sections, apply the lessons to yourself too, and make a mental note of the areas that are weak in your own language life. Encourage your children to discuss how they have been hurt by words at school or elsewhere. This helps them recognize how their words also can hurt others, even when they don't intend to be mean or insensitive.

Decide today to make your home a place that plants, nurtures, and grows good words. They don't begin in the mouth; they begin in the heart. Offer reassurances, comfort, encouragement, and loving comments freely. Fill the heart of your child with God's love and compassion. The garden that will grow will be beautiful and sustainable, and will produce great harvests that serve others with goodness.

Manners School Family Activity: Dialogue Role-Play

First things first: Are you using good words? Do your kids naturally use positive words, or do they lean toward the glass-is-half-empty attitude and the words that follow along with such negativity? It's important to know how to fill your daily conversations and your children's vocabulary with good words such as:

Please

Excuse me

I'm sorry

Thank you

With these starter words, you're off to a good start—and there are many more words and ways to transform your family's communication style. This section's family activity is intended to fuel a great discussion and demonstrate how our choice of words, language, and attitude influences every encounter we have with other people.

Here are two types of words: Words to Forget and Words to Remember. Concentrate on the "words to remember" column. Remember that the right angle for approaching a difficult problem is the "try-angle." Try out the good words on a regular basis. You'll notice a difference in your attitude and in the attitudes of those you are speaking to.

Words to Forget	Words to Remember
I can't	I can
I'll try	I will

I have to	I want to
I should have	I will do
I could have	My goal
Someday	Today
If only	Next time
Yes, but	I understand
Problem	Opportunity
Difficult	Challenging
Stressed	Motivated
Worried	Interested
Impossible	Possible
I, me, my	You, your
Hate	Love

Keep these lists in mind as you do the role-play activities. It's a great idea to write out these lists and post them in your home. That, too, could be part of this section's family activity.

Let the Role-Play Begin!

It's fun to practice and role-play with your kids. Feel free to draw from real experiences you have had in your family situation. Read these parts aloud to your kids, and let them respond as they would in the circumstance before you read the response we've provided.

What do you say when your neighbor, Mr. Smith, tells you he found your favorite baseball in his back yard?
Your child's response:
A positive response: "Thank you, Mr. Smith."

And when Mr. Smith says your baseball ruined several of his beautiful flowers?

Your child's response:

A positive response: "I'm sorry, Mr. Smith."

And when Mr. Smith asks your child if he would like to have back his baseball?

Your child's response:

A positive response: "Please, Mr. Smith."

Good words are helpful in everyday situations, especially the uncomfortable ones. That's when you really need to be on your best behavior!

Then there are the bad words. These are the words that tear down others and demean ourselves, and also the wonders of a good life. The impact of negative and hurtful words runs deep. These are the kinds of bad words we all should avoid, no matter our age:

Mean words

Teasing words

Back-talk words

Bathroom words

Bragging words

Rude words

Whispering words

Lies

Sarcastic words

Swear words

Hurtful words

Practice how to respond when others are using the bad words. This role-play time could bring up some important discussions with your children about the times they've been hurt by words or have hurt others with careless comments. Role-play the following example of negative-word scenarios.

If you are at the playground (or at school) and a friend teases another kid, what is one way you could respond?

Your child's response:

Some positive responses: You could talk directly to the friend and say, "I don't like it when you make fun of the other kids. Let's just have fun and play without bothering them. Or maybe we could include them!" Or you could respond to the child whose feelings might be hurt by saying, "I'm sorry about that. I see that you like soccer. Would you want to kick the ball with us awhile?"

If someone directs a mean comment to you, it can be tough to know how to respond. You don't want to encourage more teasing, but you also don't want to feel defeated in spirit. What would you say?

Your child's response:

A positive response: You might help the situation by saying, "Let's get along with each other. It will be more fun." Or you could address the comment directly and say, "It ruins it for everyone when you put down someone else."

Special Assignment

If your children are old enough to write out their own ideas, have them write a script that presents a situation that is first handled with the negative words. Be sure they think about what the consequences would be in that actual situation. Have them read and act out the situation.

Next, have them write another script using positive responses and language. Encourage them to show how this shift in word choices also changes the outcome of the situation. Have them read and act out this as well. Be a part of it. They might even write the script involving each family member so that everybody has a part.

The tone of your home will improve greatly when your language is elevated to positive, honest, and respectful dialogue. And a spirit of fun can thrive in an environment where attitudes are joyful.

Kid-2-Kid

Watch Your Words

Everyday manners make life easier and nicer and a lot more comfortable—and they help make special occasions more special. In fact, these everyday "dos" and "don'ts" are the heart of all other good manners.

- Do notice people's needs, and try to help. If you see a kid who has dropped a toy, pick it up. If an older person doesn't have a place to sit, offer her your seat. If someone's arms are full of books and packages, hold the door open for him.

- Do be honest. Lying and cheating are not only wrong;

they're also impolite—the very opposite of kindness and respect.

- Do show consideration for others. Being considerate means being respectful of other people's property, other people's time, and other people's rights. Cover your mouth when you sneeze and cough. Keep the noise down when others are trying to rest. Ask before using something that doesn't belong to you. Pick up after yourself.

- Don't say everything you're thinking. If you dislike your friend's new dress or you think your mom's new haircut is ugly or you notice that your teacher has a wart on her nose, you *don't* have to say it. Keep those negative thoughts to yourself.

- Don't point out other people's bad manners! This is really important. You're supposed to mind *your* manners, not your friends' manners or even your big brother's manners! It's better just to say nothing—even when someone does something really disgusting.

- Do respect others' privacy. Some things just aren't any of your business. It's impolite to read someone else's mail or diary or to look around in someone's purse, dresser drawer, or closets unless they invite you to.

- Do keep personal things personal. There are some personal things we all do (like burp, for example) that others *don't* want to watch us do or hear us talk about. If you have to do something personal, excuse yourself and go to the bathroom. Or just say a quiet "excuse me." If someone else makes a mistake, don't giggle or laugh; just ignore what happened, and don't mention it again.

- Do apologize when you need to. If you realize you have

Everyday Kindnesses in Action

said something hurtful or done something thoughtless, say "I'm sorry" or "Excuse me."

- Do show respect for grown-ups and people in authority. Parents, teachers, pastors, police officers, and other
grown-ups should be obeyed and honored. Arguing,
talking back, and being disrespectful (even behind
their backs) is bad manners.

- Do use polite words. "Please," "thank you," and "excuse
me" are like sprinkles of sugar that make all your words
and actions a little sweeter.

Tone of Voice

No matter what words come out of your mouth, your tone
of voice says a lot all by itself. When you grumble or complain,
talk down to the ground, make strange noises, grunt instead of
speaking clearly, act rudely, or avoid eye contact with the person
you are talking to—it's just plain rude.

When you aren't pleasant to be around, it shows that you
don't care about the other person and that you have better things
to do.

How to Handle Compliments

For us kids, this can be embarrassing as we often don't know
how to give a compliment or receive one from someone else.
When your favorite aunt says, "What a handsome young man
you are!" for the third time at the Christmas dinner, it can be
kind of awkward. Everyone's looking at you, so how do you act?
The best thing to do is smile and say, "Thank you," and hope
someone changes the subject. If you want to give someone else a
compliment, go ahead and do it. Compliments make other people

49

feel good about themselves. Just make sure you really mean what you say, and try not to overdo it!

How You Say It

You've probably heard, "It's not what you say that counts, but how you say it." Often you will express yourself differently when you are talking to one person than when you are speaking to a larger group. Body language, more than what you say, tells listeners about you. Watch your smile, your eyes, your clinching of fists and arms, how you position your body when you are speaking. Depending on the occasion, the way you act can be casual or more formal.

Watch what you say. It's fine to change the way you talk to fit the group you're with. And you shouldn't ever make up stuff to impress other people or act like someone you're not.

If You're Stuck

If you find yourself stuck and aren't sure what to say or do, try to remember the Golden Rule. Do you like it when others make fun of you? Probably not! Would you like for other people to think you are smart and handsome and that your skateboard is cool? Sure you would! So remember—before you say something, ask yourself, *Would I want to hear this to my face?* If the answer is no, you'd better not say anything. If it's yes, go ahead and say it. Just be careful and watch your words—they do count.

When to Talk

Did you know that sometimes it's best not to talk at all? Here's a good rule to remember: When you're talking to someone, you should listen at least as much as you talk.

If the person you're talking to is shy, ask him some questions about himself. Just make sure they're not questions that can be answered with a simple yes or no. This should get them talking in no time, and you'll learn a lot about your new friend.

Kid-2-Kid

How to Talk to Big People

If you're like most kids, having a conversation with an adult can be a real stretch. It's hard to think of things to say to Mrs. Doodlebug across the street, Grandpa Joe calling on the phone from across the country, or even Bruce, the chatty cashier at the grocery store. You might get really quiet and shy, even though you're *not* that way with your friends. Or you might talk so much that people think you're a total blabbermouth. With good manners, you can still be yourself *and* have fun talking to grown-ups.

Beginning a Conversation

Let's begin with the basics here. First off, say hello and greet people when you meet them. Use their names. It makes people feel good, and it also gives you practice in remembering who's who. After all, don't you hate it when people forget your name? If you've forgotten someone's name, it's okay to say, "I'm sorry, but I can't remember your name." Make eye contact with the person you are talking to. Stand up to greet her, and let her have the best seat or give them a place in line ahead of you. And it's best not to interrupt grown-ups who are talking, unless, of course, it's an emergency.

Kids used to always call adults by their title and last name, like Mrs. Bananapeel or Mr. Washcloth. That was just how it was done. But things are a little different these days. For instance, your friend Weston's dad wants you to call him Brad. There's nothing wrong with that, but it might be more comfortable for you to call him Mr. Brad.

Always call adults by their title and last name (Mrs. Multiplication, Dr. Influenza) unless they ask you to do otherwise. It's a sign of respect. And, of course, just about anything is better than "Hey, you!"

Talking to Strangers

It's important to be friendly and to speak up, but it's also important to be safe. Discuss with your parents when you may and when you should not strike up a conversation with an adult stranger. For example, if you are at the playground and an adult approaches you, your parents might prefer that you come to get them before talking to that adult. But if you are all at a gathering together, such as your dad's company picnic or a church potluck, and you are near an adult you don't know, your parents might agree that it shows good manners to say: "My name is _____; I have not met you before, but I would like to introduce myself to you." Most adults would be very impressed to meet a young person who would have the confidence to do that.

If you are scared, or if you are at all worried about whether it is a safe situation, just find one of your parents or another adult whom you and your family trusts. You could then take that person over with you to meet the other adult and to make introductions.

Knowing What to Say

You've been invited to spend the night at Bradley Joe's house.

He told you to come by at seven, but he's not home from basketball practice yet. You're sitting in the living room with his parents, feeling kind of awkward. Don't bolt for home just yet. Bradley Joe's folks will probably ask you some questions. When they ask if you like sports, don't just reply, "Yes." Give a little more information—"Yes, I like soccer the best. I play defender on the Westside Walruses." And ask *them* some questions too! They're probably interested in some of the same things you like—sports, food, things happening at your school.

The Phone

There goes the phone again, and you're the one closest to it. Even if answering the phone isn't your favorite thing to do—it's *never* for you—you still need to use good manners. So here's what you do. First, say "hello" (not "yeah" or "whaddaya want"). If it's actually for you—great! Then you just talk. If it's for your sister Maria, ask the person on the other end to please wait while you call her to the phone. And don't just stand there and scream, "Maria! Phone!" You don't want to blast anyone's ears out. If Maria isn't home, be sure to write down the message and leave it where she will find it. If you're calling Bevan and his mom answers, tell her who you are. If Bevan isn't home, leave an easy, short message. And if you get an answering machine, be sure to leave a message on it; don't just hang up.

Using text messaging has become the new wave of communication, particularly with us younger members of society. Text messaging is rude when a person does it instead of being present for what is happening around him or her.

There's no denying that text messaging is very much a part of our culture now. It can be very useful when you need to communicate quick facts or updates to others and you don't have time for an entire phone conversation. Always keep your texts brief, just a few lines, and follow up with a phone call if you need to add more information. Here are a few abbreviations that you can use to shorten messages:

- FWIW: for what it's worth
- IIRC: if I recall correctly
- HTH: happy to help/hope that helps
- TIA: thanks in advance
- FYI: for your information
- BTW: by the way
- OBO: our best offer
- TTYL: talk to you later
- BCNU: be seeing you
- CU2MO: see you tomorrow
- IMHO: in my humble opinion

And there's more. The following symbols are known as smileys:

- :-) = smiling
- :-(= frowning
- :-D = surprised
- :-/ = perplexed

Smileys enable you to communicate how you feel about a subject. They can appear to be flippant, so be really sure you're sending them to a person who is sure to understand and appreciate them.

Using e-mail lets you send an immediate message from one part of the world to another part of the world without having to add a postage stamp on the envelope. This form of communication has its good-news aspect and its bad-news aspect. The good news is that you can quickly send a message to a friend or to your grandmother. The bad news is that your e-mail inbox can be flooded with all kinds of junk. Many folks complain that they have to sift through dozens of entries before they find a meaningful message. Think before you send a mass e-mail to a group of friends. And don't develop a reputation of sending out inappropriate stories and jokes.

Never use e-mail for sending a thank-you note to someone who has given you a gift. Nothing can substitute for a handwritten note or letter.

Adults You Don't Know

When you talk to adults when you're out and about—like waiters and waitresses or delivery people—it's important to be nice and polite. But keep in mind that you don't have to say a whole lot to them (besides "please" and "thank you.") If you're with your parents or other grown-ups, just follow their lead. Sometimes adults you don't know, such as salespeople, come to your door. It's best not to let any stranger inside your house. If you're home alone, you don't even have to answer the door. And *never* say that you're home alone. (Don't say this on the phone, either.) Just tell the person that your mom or dad can't come to the door or phone right now and that you'll give them a message.

Ho, Hum...

You're in a roomful of adults, and you're totally bored out of your mind. Is it okay to just leave the room? If you're at home and you have something you really need to take care of, like doing your homework or feeding the dog, quietly tell your parents and ask if you may be excused. If your parents think it's important that you stay, however, you're stuck. Make the best of the situation by keeping busy (getting drinks for people, gathering up dishes). You can also pretend that you'll be tested on what people are talking about. See how much you can remember.

*Always keep your words soft and sweet—
one day you might have to eat them.*

Kid-2-Kid

Happy to Meet You

I love to talk! Don't you?

But have you ever noticed that sometimes the beginning or ending of a conversation is harder than the middle?

Sometimes when I meet someone new, I feel all tongue-tied. Sometimes I feel grumpy and don't want to say anything (especially to my brother in the morning!). Sometimes I'm so excited and happy I don't even know what to say.

Then sometimes, when it's time to go, I don't know how to *end* a conversation, either. That's when manners come to the rescue.

If you've practiced a nice, polite way to meet and greet people, you can get to that fun middle of a conversation without worrying too much about the beginning and the end.

Starting Off

It's always nice to stand to say hello, *especially* if I'm meeting somebody older than me. Then I smile, look at the person, shake hands, and say something like:

"Hello"

or

"How are you this morning?"

A friendly "Hi" is all right, too, especially if I'm meeting someone my age. I usually like to say the other person's name out loud. This lets him know I remember who he is and usually makes the person feel good. If I've just met someone, saying the name out loud helps me remember it!

When I meet Aunt Jenny, I always give her a big hug instead of shaking hands. I try to hug my parents a lot, too, especially when we haven't seen each other all day. When I see my brother in the morning, sometimes all I can manage is "Good morning," but that's important too. I do the same with my friends.

It's nice to say "Good morning" and "How are you" even to people you see every day and even when you're busy. Taking the time to say a friendly hello is really a way of saying, "You're important. I care about you."

Introducing People

Conversations are always more fun if everyone knows everybody else. If someone is new, it's good to introduce him. And it's nice to say something to help the people know each other a little better.

I just say something like:

"Aunt Jenny, this is my friend, Chad. We go to school together."

or

"Donna, this is Anne. She lives down the street from me, and we go to church together."

It's polite to introduce younger people to older ones, and introduce boys to girls. This means that I say the older person's or the girl's name first:

"Mrs. Klein, this is my friend Christine."

or

"Eileen, this is Bradley Joe."

What if a lot of people in a group don't know the new person? I just say something to the whole group like,

"Everybody, this is Yoli Brogger. She just moved in next door to me."

Then, if the group is small, I go around the circle and tell the new person the names of all the others. If it's a really big group, like my class in school, I might ask them to tell her their names themselves. Then I stick around to make sure people are talking to the new person and to help her fit in.

Meeting-and-greeting manners are about speaking up, pleasantly, and making sure everybody knows everybody else.

Introducing Yourself

If I meet someone new and no one introduces the person to me, I'm learning just to go ahead and introduce myself. That's kind of hard sometimes. I keep waiting for the other person to say hello. But if both of us are waiting like that, we might never meet each other!

It's really a lot better just to smile and say, "Hi. I'm Emilie Marie. What's your name?"

If I'm greeting someone I met a long time ago but haven't seen in a while (like my kindergarten teacher), it's still important to say my name. It's just not fair to say, "Hi, remember me?"—she might be embarrassed if she doesn't. So I just give a little reminder:

"Hi, I'm Emilie Marie. I was in your kindergarten class five years ago. I'm glad to see you again."

Practice introducing yourself to your family members. You can even get silly by making up names and situations as you role-play. Just be sure to practice a few times using your real name so it becomes easy to do when you are actually introducing yourself to a stranger or to someone you don't know very well.

Breaking the Ice

When I'm talking to people I don't know very well, sometimes it's hard to know what to talk about after the hellos are finished. Aunt Jenny says the very best way to handle this is to remember that most people like to talk about themselves. So I just ask questions and listen to the answers in a friendly way. I mean general, get-to-know-you questions, like:

"Do you have any hobbies?"

"Do you like animals?"

"Where did you go to school last year?"

Asking questions is a good way to get a conversation started. Aunt Jenny calls it "breaking the ice," and it's a good way to start talking to almost anyone.

A Friendly Chat

After the ice is broken and we're right in the middle of talking, there are still some things I can do to keep the conversation fun and pleasant for everyone.

One important thing is to include everyone in the conversation. Whispering to one person in front of somebody else is really impolite, even if it's a very important secret and not mean at all. The people you're not whispering to may feel left out, and they may wonder if you're talking about them.

Another important thing to do when you're talking is to listen. A conversation is not just what you say, but what others say, and it's hard to be a good listener if you're always interrupting or thinking about what you want to say next.

Sometimes I'll get so excited that an idea will just blurt out while someone else is still talking. The thing to do then is to say:

"Oh, excuse me. I didn't mean to interrupt."

"I'm sorry. Go ahead."

And sometimes (especially with grown-ups) it seems like the other person will *never* stop talking so I can say something. If it's really an emergency, I might interrupt with a very polite:

"Excuse me, but the house is on fire."

Otherwise, it's best to hold my thought until they're through. (I usually *do* get my turn.)

Of course, that reminds me of something else it's important to do in a pleasant conversation—which is to give everyone a chance to talk! I hope I remember that when I'm a grown-up.

Acting interested in the conversation is another kind of good manners. This is easy when I'm talking with my friends, but not always easy when I'm talking with older people or people I don't find interesting. Even if I'm bored, it's not polite to yawn or look all around while someone is talking. (I wouldn't like it if someone did that to me!) When someone asks me a question, it's much nicer to answer with something more than "Uh-huh" or "uh-uh."

When it is my turn to talk, there are certain kinds of things it is better *not* to say. Aunt Jenny calls this being tactful, and it simply means I don't say everything I'm thinking, especially if what I'm thinking might hurt someone's feelings. I don't tell Grandma she's fat. I don't blurt out that Suzie walks funny. I don't tell about the embarrassing thing that happened to my mom.

Saying Goodbye

When it's time to say goodbye, there's not really any need to hang around. All I need to say is:

"Bye."

"See you."

"Thanks. It was fun talking to you."

If the conversation just won't stop and I really need to leave, I can interrupt politely:

"Excuse me, but my mom's here. I've got to go. Goodbye."

I also like to tell new people I'm glad I met them. Just a few simple words will do it, like:

"Goodbye, it was really nice to meet you."

or

"I hope I see you again."

And you know what? When I've been using my manners, I usually mean just that!

Don't Make a Big Deal About It

If I notice something embarrassing the other person does not know—maybe she has something caught in her teeth or a big stain on the back of her shirt—I don't mention it in public. I wait until we're alone and tell her in a quiet, friendly voice. Sometimes I might say, "Excuse me, could I talk to you over here," but I don't make a big deal about it. That could be even more embarrassing than the teeth or the stain.

Talk, Talk, Talk, We All Love to Talk

Telephone talk is really just like any other talk—except that you and the other person can't see each other. You can't use a friendly smile or an interested face to help you say what you want to say. All you have are your words and your voice to give a message that is clear and friendly.

Aunt Jenny says that's the heart of telephone manners. What I say over the phone should put a smile in the other person's heart!

As a kid, it is very important to answer the phone with energy and enthusiasm. Probably the other caller will draw an opinion of what kind of a young person you are by the way you answer the phone.

Ring-a-Ding-Ding

What do I do when the phone rings? First, I say hello (not "yeah" or "whaddaya want"). It's nice to say who I am too:

"Hello. This is Emilie Marie speaking."

If it's for me—hooray! Then I just talk. If it's for someone else, I politely ask the person on the telephone to wait while I call the other person to the phone.

"Just a minute, please. I'll get him...Bob, it's for you."

How I call Bob is really important. It's rude to just stand there and yell. The person who called will get her ears blasted, and besides, nobody likes to be yelled at! It's better to cover the mouthpiece (the part I speak into) with my hand and ask Bob quietly to come to the phone. If he's in the other room, I should put the phone down and go find him.

Aunt Jenny says it's helpful to ask who is calling. That way, the person the call is for can get ready for the conversation and greet the caller by name. But just blurting out, "Who is this?" is not a polite way to ask. It's better to say:

"May I tell him who's calling?" or

"Who is calling, please?"

If I know the person who is calling, even if she's not calling to talk to me, it's always nice to talk a little before I go to find the person she called:

"Good morning, Mrs. Brogger. How are you? I'm fine. I'll go get Mom now."

What if the person the call is for isn't home? Then I offer to take a message. I find a piece of paper, write down the message, and put it where the person will find it. (In our house we keep a little notepad and a pencil by the phone.) But even if I took a message, I tell the person about the call when I see her...just in case she didn't see the paper.

When You Are the Caller

When I'm the person making the call, I try to give the other person plenty of time to get to the phone. Aunt Jenny says I should let the phone ring at least five or six times before I give up.

When somebody answers the phone, the first thing I do is say who I am—remember, the person can't see me, and it's not fair to make her guess!

"Hello, this is Emilie Marie Barnes."

I always give my full name unless I'm absolutely positive the other person knows who I am. (There are three Samanthas in my class, so there might be other Emilie Maries as well!) Then I ask politely for the person I want to speak to:

"May I speak to Danny, please?"

If the person I am calling is not home, I usually leave a message—an easy, short one! Once I left a long, complicated message for my friend Janet, and her brother got it all mixed up—what a mess! So now I usually just leave my phone number.

Leaving a message on an answering machine isn't really any different from leaving a message with someone's mom or dad or brother or sister—except the machine doesn't make as many mistakes! I just wait for the beep (like the message tells me), give my name and the name of the person I'm calling, and leave my number and message.

"Hello, this is Emilie Marie, and I'm calling for Bob. Please call me back when you can. My number is 555-4000."

Aunt Jenny says I should always leave some sort of message on an answering machine, even if I dialed the wrong number and got someone else's machine, but I should keep all my messages short. And when I'm through leaving my message, it's always nice to say "thank you" and "goodbye" so the person knows the message is finished—and to leave him or her with a nice feeling.

Wrong-Number Calls

When the phone rings, I always hope it's someone I like. But sometimes it's a total stranger calling for someone I never heard of—it's a wrong number. Anyone can make a mistake, including me. So I try to be friendly and helpful to wrong-number callers. I say something like:

"I'm sorry, you must have dialed the wrong number. What number were you calling?"

Then, when the caller says "I'm sorry," I say, "That's all right. Goodbye."

If the caller just hangs up on me, I think, *How rude!* But that helps me remember not to just hang up when I dial a wrong number.

It's important always to say "I'm sorry" and "thank you." Sometimes I tell the person the number I was calling—I can figure out if the number I have is wrong or if my fingers just slipped:

"Oh, I'm sorry. I was dialing 555-4500. Is that your number?"

One thing I shouldn't do if someone calls my number by mistake is give him my name or phone number. That's like giving my name to a stranger, and it's just not a good idea.

First Person First

Do you have call-waiting on your phone? We do in our house, and cell phones all receive second calls. If I'm on the phone and someone else tries to call our number, I hear a little beep in my ear. If I want to, I can put the first person "on hold" while I answer the new call. My mom showed me how to do it. I just press quickly on the little button that hangs up the phone, and then I can answer the other call.

Call-waiting is nice when a really important call comes in—like my dad calling to say he'll be late. But call-waiting can be a problem if I make the first person wait a long time while I talk to the second one. That's a little like letting someone cut in line.

There's another kind of "call waiting" that happens sometimes when I'm at a friend's house. We can be playing together, having a good time, when someone calls her on the phone. And then she has a long talk with that other person while I just sit there! That makes me feel like I'm not very important to my friend.

Aunt Jenny and I have decided on a manners rule that takes care of both of these waiting problems. "First person first." That means the first person I am talking to—on the phone or in person—gets most of my attention. If anyone else calls, I'll talk just long enough to write down her number so I can call her back later. Of course, if the second call is an emergency or someone you really need to talk to, there's nothing wrong with saying to the first person:

"I'm sorry, but this is a really important call. Do you mind if I call you later to talk?"

Good manners help us think about how other people feel—and then do what we can to make them feel important and respected.

Using the Phone Properly

Speaking clearly and distinctly is a very important part of telephone manners. So is using polite words like "please" and "thank you." Listening carefully and not interrupting is most important of all.

Reading or watching TV—in other words, not really listening—while you're on the phone is very rude. So is interrupting a phone conversation to speak to someone who is with you in the room. How can the person on the phone know who you are talking to? If you don't understand something, you should always say, "I beg your pardon," or, "I'm sorry, I didn't understand that."

Some kids I know like to play pranks and jokes on the phone—like answering the phone in a silly way or calling up someone they don't know and asking joke questions or hanging up on people. Jokes like these aren't funny at all. They waste other people's time, and sometimes they are even hurtful. It's a lot more fun and helpful to use your creativity to do good things.

Sharing the Telephone

In our family, we have four people and three telephones, but only one telephone line—and sometimes, more than one of us wants to use the phone at the same time. Sharing a phone with other people means we have to be considerate of one another's needs.

Being considerate about using the phone means not talking too long when someone else needs to make a call.

It means not making a big fuss about waiting for someone else to get off the phone—and saying thank you when they do.

It means taking down messages carefully and remembering to deliver them.

It means asking your mom or dad before making calls that cost extra—such as long distance.

It especially means not listening in secretly on one phone while your brother or sister is talking on the other one—even when the conversation is really interesting.

And when your family has cell phones and you share minutes, be sure you respect whatever rules your parents have set. Cell phones are a privilege and are very useful for emergencies and for keeping a family connected. If your parents decide to provide you with a cell phone at a certain age, treat the phone and the use of the phone with respect. Show your family how responsible you can be, and you'll have more opportunities and freedoms later.

A Little Bit Bashful

What do you do when you don't know what to say over the phone?

Talking to my friends or my parents or Aunt Jenny is easy. But sometimes I get confused or shy when I talk to grown-ups and people I don't know very well. I don't know what to say, so I just sit there.

Aunt Jenny says that happens to everyone sometimes, but it's really important to learn to talk pleasantly with people I don't know. The talk doesn't have to be long, but it has to be more than just some grumbles and grunts.

It helps to practice, so Aunt Jenny and I have pretend conversations. It also helps to write down a list of things to talk about over the phone. I did that with Grandma. I wrote down some things to tell her and some things to ask her about, and I put my list by the phone.

And you know what? The more we talk on the phone, the better I know her, and the less tongue-tied I feel. Now we have a lot of good talks on the telephone—just like I have with my friends.

That's the best thing about the telephone, I think.

It's a really good way to keep up with old friends, and make new friends too.

And all that works a lot better when I remember to practice my telephone manners.

When Your Parents Are Gone

I and all my friends know it's not a good idea ever to tell a caller we're home by ourselves. But what do you say?

My mom always told me just to say, "I'm sorry. She can't come to the phone right now. I'll be glad to take a message." I don't need to fib and say something like, "Oh, my mom's in the shower." It's best just to be polite, grown-up, and calm.

Want in on a phone secret? Smiling while you talk on the telephone makes your voice sound friendlier. Some people put a sign (SMILE) near where their phone is as a reminder. It really works.

The heart of manners is always the same: showing kindness and respect for others. So when your parents trust you to be home alone, you'll want to be sure to respect all the house rules, even though nobody is there to see what you are doing. Don't be on the phone for hours when the house rule is to keep conversations brief. Only call the friends your parents know and have met or have said you can communicate with. And never pursue a phone conversation with someone you don't know.

Thanks a Lot

"Thank you" is a magic manners phrase. It makes everyone feel better: both the person who's being thanked *and* the person saying thank you. In fact, did you know that it's impossible to have too much thanks in our lives? That's right! So you can never go overboard saying, "Thanks a bunch!"

Saying Thanks

When is a good time to say thank you? Whenever anyone gives you a compliment, helps you with a project or does you a favor, has you over to her house for dinner or to spend the night, takes you someplace fun, or invites you to a party. And, of course, it's always good manners to thank anyone who gives you a gift.

Sometimes it's fine to say thank you in person, and other times you should write a thank-you note. How do you know when to do what? If someone has sent you a gift or done something especially nice, you need to send that person a written thank-you note. Some people today think thank-you notes are old-fashioned. They say it's easier to say thanks in person or call the giver on the phone. But a written note is really nice. It's like giving a gift back to the person who did something for you. And thank-you notes also help ensure that the person who did the nice thing or gave the great gift will do something for you again!

E-mails and text messaging are not okay ways to send a thank-you response. I know it's the modern-technology way, but you can't beat the old-fashioned handwritten thank-you note.

When Do I Write It?

It's important to write thank-you notes as soon as possible after receiving the gift or getting home from the party. If you wait too long, you may forget to write it at all! So try to write it within the week. But if you forget until a month or two later, go ahead and write the thank-you note anyway. It's always better to send a late note than no note at all!

A thank-you note also lets the sender of a gift know that you received the gift.

How Do I Say It?

This is the hard part of writing thank-you notes—knowing what to say. For Christmas or birthdays, when you receive lots of gifts from lots of people, keep a list of who gave you what. That way you won't get confused, trying to remember who gave you the orange-and-green polka-dot sweater and who gave you the purple-and-red striped socks. When you write the note, mention the gift by name, and talk about how much you appreciate the time and effort the person put into either making or buying it. You should also talk about how you used the gift or might want to use it. You can add a little news about your life, especially for people who live far away. Thank-you notes don't have to be very long at all. When you're done writing your thank-you notes, give yourself a reward like a bike ride or a plate of chocolate chip cookies. (You can also have a smaller reward halfway through, like *half* a plate of cookies.) Here's an example of a thank-you note:

> Dear Grammy:
>
> Thank you for the stocking cap and matching mittens. It's always so nice of you to make gifts for all of your grandchildren. That must take a lot of time! Thanks for working so hard for me. I'm looking forward to seeing you this Christmas. Dad says we are supposed to get a lot of snow. I'm excited!
>
> Love, Christine

Even When You Don't Like It

An expression of thanks is always important, even when you get a gift that isn't exactly everything you dreamed of! You know your Grammy loves you and that she means well, but every Christmas she gives you a gift that makes you wonder if she's lost it. This year it's a really ugly neon yellow, bright purple, and lime green stocking cap with a big pom-pom on top and a matching pair of mittens. So how do you thank someone for something you don't like very much?

You need to find something about the gift you really are thankful for—even if it's just the fact that the other person cared enough to give you a gift!

> *The most significant change in*
> *a person's life is a change of attitude.*
> *Right attitudes produce right actions.*
>
> WILLIAM JOHNSON

The Satisfaction of Social Graces

Manners Open the Door to the Heart and the Home

*Life be not so short but that there
is always time for courtesy.*

RALPH WALDO EMERSON

Manners begin at the front door and then extend into the home, where they are taught, modeled, and expressed. The pleasing home is not measured by perfection; it is measured by the foundation of gracious style you've laid. A neat—not perfect, but neat—home may have a potted flowering plant out front and a swept walkway. Anything that is warm, cheerful, and inviting will be a welcome sign to guests and family alike. When you take care of your home, those who live there and those who visit know that they, too, will be cared for.

My guests love to walk into my home when something is cooking on the stove. The rich aroma of food invites the guest beyond the front door. If nothing else, try boiling a few cinnamon sticks in a pot of hot water. This will at least lead your friends to believe you are domestic.

The personality of a welcoming home makes guests want to linger, regardless of whether that home is a hut or a palace. Don't feel as if your home has to be decorated exactly the way you want it in order to express a personality that beckons with open arms. Remember, a home is always in process. If you wait to invite guests until it is the way you want it, you will never have guests. People love you for who you are and not for what your home looks like.

Children Can Be Big Helpers

Don't feel that your home has to be all about Mom and Dad. Children play a large part in making guests feel welcomed in your home. Since the family is made up of several people, several people should help make home an enjoyable setting. They certainly can make others feel welcome when they come for a visit.

Children are very capable of helping Mom and Dad get ready for guests. You might write out on a piece of paper individual assignments for each of the children. Children love to feel that they are valuable parts of the family. Be sure to praise them when they have completed their assignments.

How Children Can Help

- Be responsible for keeping their bedrooms in order.
- Help pick up any toys that may be scattered around the rooms.

Ding-Dong the Doorbell Rings

- Properly greet guests at the door.

- Assist in taking any coats or purses, putting them all in an easy location.

- Introduce guests to the rest of the family—make sure everyone knows each other.

- Offer them something to drink.

- Escort them to the living room and offer them a place to sit.

- Have place cards present on the dining room table so your company will know where to sit.

- If the gathering is outdoors, children can escort guests to the patio, deck, or yard and direct them toward the beverages or seating that is available.

- For gatherings that will take place at the dining table, children can help prearrange the placement of your guests around the table so strangers will get to know others easily.

- Practice table manners from start to finish. After your family has studied the dining section of this book, the kids will be able to eat with gracious manners while engaging in polite, inviting conversation.

- At the end of the visit, children should return to where the adults are gathered and say goodbye as your guests leave your home.

Well-mannered children are a real blessing. Other adults love to be in the presence of children who have some social graces.

If you want a lesson in creating a welcoming home, the best classroom you can visit is the South. This culture has earned and deserves the "Southern hospitality" reputation. I've had the good fortune to visit Charleston, South Carolina, and Savannah,

Georgia, and both cities seemed to say, "Welcome to our lifestyle." The South shines as a model of grace, charm, and hospitality. It's a place where people even slow down a bit to enjoy the ritual of afternoon tea—one of my favorite things! This section of the country still honors social poise and presentation. Grandmother's china cups and silver elements are still reverenced in the home. The table isn't covered with plastic and paper goods. And table manners are alive and well even among the young.

The ingredients of hospitality and social graces go together regardless of where you live. You might use different elements and different languages, but wherever you are, don't forget these two ingredients.

When you entertain, practice proper etiquette and manners before you send out your invitations. People take notice and will learn from you how to handle yourself in these situations. These settings are great learning situations for your children too. We all have to sharpen our social skills. At each gathering we have a chance to learn something new—something valuable to use later.

Having company provides a wonderful opportunity for old friends and new friends to come together. It's also a great time for the whole family to review a few of the important manners so your family puts its best foot forward.

Manners School Family Activity: Welcoming Guests by Name

Add an extra personal welcome to your table by using place cards. Each card features an individual's name and lets that guest know where to sit. This touch of hospitality is simple and yet it removes the awkwardness of a guest's having to figure out where she should sit. People are afraid they'll take a spot preferred by another. Or that they'll sit in the seat one of the host family members always sits in. And in a subtle, helpful way, place cards send a message to the guests that they were thought of personally in advance of the meal, and are regarded with such care that you want them to have special, specific places at the table. What a comfort that is, especially to someone who is visiting your home for the first time or who doesn't know the other people attending a gathering.

The cards are usually placed above the dinner plate at each person's place. Some hostesses put them on top of the napkin on the dinner plate. The place card is usually plain white, about an inch and a half high by two inches long. There's no exact size recommended. Use your best penmanship to print your guests' names on the cards.

If you have guests who may not know one another, place cards can be helpful to remind them of the first names of those sitting beside them. Even after proper introductions have been made, it's easy to forget a new name.

If you'd like to add a personal touch for an upcoming event, try making these homemade place cards as your manners school family activity. In fact, you should plan on making these so that you have a set for the family. It's fun for everyone.

Homemade Place Cards

These salt dough place cards are fun to make and a joy to present to friends and family at a gathering. Follow the recipe, and invite loved ones to a time of fellowship, conversation, and the pleasures of friendship.

2 cups flour

1 cup salt

½ to 1 cup water

Mix flour and salt. Add water a tablespoon at a time until mixture forms a kneadable dough. Turn out onto a lightly floured surface and knead for about ten minutes. Roll out to a 3/8-inch thickness. Use cookie cutters to cut dough into desired shapes for the place cards. In addition, for each two place cards, cut a 2 x 4 inch rectangle out of the rolled dough. Cut the rectangle from corner to corner to make two long triangles. These will be the props that hold the place cards upright. Place all the cutouts on a cookie sheet and bake in a very low oven (150 to 200 degrees) until completely hard—at least several hours. When the dough has cooled completely, paint the place cards with acrylic paint and then paint the guest's name on top. Let paint dry—then spray front and back with several layers of polyurethane varnish. Spray the triangular cutouts as well. When all is dry, use a hot-glue gun to attach the two-inch edge of the triangle to the bottom of the place cards.

If you want the place cards to lean back slightly, experiment with the shape of the prop. If you trim the two-inch edge at a little more of an angle, the place card will lean back just a bit, showing off the name and graciously inviting friends to the table.

Kid-2-Kid

Everyone Loves a Party

"It's time for a party!"

Those are words I'm always happy to hear.

Sometimes I'm the party giver. And sometimes I'm a party-goer. Either way, parties are fun—and they're a great place to practice good manners.

Party-time manners are not really hard to learn. Mostly they're just everyday good manners and mealtime manners and visiting manners all combined with an extra spark—making sure everyone has a special good time.

Making Party Plans

If I want to give a party of my own, the first thing I need to do is check with my parents and maybe some other adults. Not only is this polite, but I need their permission and their help! We need to talk together about what kind of party it will be, where it will be held, and how many people I can invite.

Once those important things have been decided, I can start planning. I really like this part of being a party giver.

First, I need to think about party food and decorations and games. I need to pick a theme and decide whether the party will be at home or somewhere else, like a park or a restaurant. Parties at pizza places, amusement parks, or gymnastics places are very popular. But I think that home parties can be even more fun—that way I actually get to spend more time with my friends.

Sometimes I like to have a very small tea party with just four or five guests. (I've even had tea parties for two.) Other times I invite a bigger group. I think it's fun to invite people I know from different places and help them get to know one another too.

If my party is going to be small, I usually just invite a few of my good friends. If it's big, I try to invite all of one group of people—my whole Brownie troop or all the girls in my class. That way people's feelings don't get hurt by being left out.

Boys and girls parties are very different. Girls like fluff and lace, and boys like noise and high energy. The theme may be different, but the planning is almost the same.

Please Come

If my party is going to be very casual, like a sleepover with a few friends, I usually just call them on the phone and invite them—or sometimes my mom calls their moms.

For a bigger or fancier party, though, it's better to send out written invitations. These can be plain or fancy, cute or serious, and I can make them by hand or fill in the "blanks" on ready-printed invitations. I usually like to make my own because it's fun. I fold a piece of construction paper, cut it in a fancy shape without cutting through the fold, decorate the outside, and then write the invitation on the inside.

Aunt Jenny says that for some occasions, when I am older—like graduations and my wedding—I will want to send out formal engraved invitations. That means they are printed in a special way following certain special rules. For now, though, all I really need to worry about is making sure my invitations tell my friends what they need to know. An invitation should tell who is giving the party (me), what kind of party it will be, when the party will be held, and where it will be. It can also tell about special clothes guests should wear and things they should bring, and whether they need to tell me they are coming.

It's usually best to send the invitations through the mail. I can also pass them out by hand if I am absolutely certain that someone won't see someone else get an invitation and feel left out.

Once the invitations have gone out, it's time to plan.

A party is usually more fun with games, and games usually

help guests get to know one another better. Sometimes I like to have silly games where everyone gets active. Other times we play guessing games or just talk. One time we even acted out a story! The most important thing about a party game is that everyone should be able to take part.

Food for a party can be almost anything. Ice cream and cake is usual for a birthday party, but I had a friend who had a birthday watermelon, complete with candles! I can serve my guests pretzels and soda, or we can have a complete meal. But I need to think ahead to make sure I'll have enough for everybody and also that everyone will have a place to sit while they eat. (Aunt Jenny always says that half of what makes a party fun is careful planning.)

Mom and Dad and I always work together to make the food and put up the decorations. (I help them when they have parties too.) And, of course, I pitch in to get the house looking nice and clean. It's not fair (and not polite) to have all the fun and leave Mom and Dad with all the work!

It's Party Time!

When the time for my party finally rolls around, sometimes I feel nervous. Aunt Jenny says it's all right to feel this way. That just means I care about my guests and my party and want everyone to have fun.

She must be right. We always seem to have fun!

I want to make sure everybody at my party feels special. I greet all my guests at the door and make sure they know everybody else. If someone has brought a gift (either because it's a birthday party or just to be nice), I say a big thank you, and I set it aside till later. Then I show my guests around and try to make sure they feel welcome.

Once everyone is there, I try to make sure no one feels left out. If I spot someone standing alone in a corner, I go over and talk to her. I explain the games and let everyone know what there is to eat or drink. And even though it is my party and I planned it, I try not to act bossy and tell everyone what to do. If my party is a birthday party, there will probably be a time when I open the presents my friends have brought me. There's a nice way to do this. With each present, say out loud who it's from, read any card, then open the present and hold it up so that everyone can see. Then I say another great big thank you (and I'll write a thank-you note later).

When it's time for the party to end, I always go to the door with each guest as she leaves. I thank my guests for coming and thank them again for any gifts they brought.

I also like to give the guests at my party little favors or gifts to help them remember my party. These don't have to be fancy or expensive, but they should be a way to tell them, "Thanks for coming. I'm really glad you did."

When I'm Invited

If I'm the one invited to a party, the first thing I need to do is respond promptly to the invitation—to say yes or no. (It's nice to do this even if the invitation doesn't say RSVP.) If the party giver invites me by phone, I can just answer right then or call her back to give an answer.

If the invitation was written, I need to call the phone number on the card. It's not enough just to see the party giver in the hall at school and say, "I want to come."

If the invitation is for a birthday party, of course, I'll usually want to bring a present. For a casual party with friends, it's all right just to bring myself...and a fun attitude.

What should I wear to a party? Sometimes the invitation will say "casual," "dressy," or even "costume." Or sometimes the kind of party it is will tell me what to do. (I would never wear a frilly dress to go horseback riding.) If I'm not sure, the best thing to do is call the friend who is giving the party and ask!

How to Be a Good Partygoer

When the day of the party arrives, my most important job is to have a good time. But I can also do a lot to help others have a good time, too, and help the party go smoothly. And, of course, I want to make my host and hostesses feel glad they invited me.

If it's a birthday party, I should say, "Happy birthday" to the guest of honor as I hand over my gift.

After that, I should introduce myself to people I don't know and talk to people who look lonely. It's important to participate happily in the games and activities and to be a good sport if I lose. I don't complain about the food, the favors, or anything else.

Although parties are famous for having fun food, that doesn't mean I should forget my mealtime manners. In fact, I think nice manners make a party special, so I always try to pay attention to sitting up straight, chewing with my mouth closed, and eating neatly. I try not to load up my plate, especially if others haven't been served yet.

Sometimes I feel nervous at a party, especially if I don't know everyone. Aunt Jenny says I can help that nervous feeling by looking for someone else who looks a little lost and talking to her. I can also offer to help my hostess pass out food or drinks—having something to do helps with those nervous butterflies.

What if I do something embarrassing at a party? What if I spill something or trip somebody or break something? I need to remember that accidents can happen to anybody. I should simply apologize and maybe help my host or hostess clean up the mess. If I've broken something or stained something, it's polite to ask if I can help pay for it. But once the problem is taken care of, I should forget about it. I don't want to ruin the party talking on and on about a problem!

Finally, when it's time to go, I make sure I find my host and her parents and say that I had a good time. Then when I get home, it's nice to write a note or card that says another thank you.

Grown-up Parties and Family Parties

Not every party I go to involves just kids. Sometimes I help at grown-up parties my parents give. Sometimes we go together to parties where there are both adults and children. Once I was the flower girl at a wedding, and I got to go to the rehearsal dinner and the reception. (That was really fun—I even caught the bouquet!)

If the party is at my house, I like to help greet the guests and take their coats. I also help serve the food and clean up, and I try to entertain any kids who have come to the party, even young ones. If the party goes past my bedtime, I usually just say a polite goodnight to everyone and go to my room (or sometimes my parents let me stay up until everyone leaves).

If I am a guest at a grown-up party, I try not to be loud or rowdy. I speak politely when I am spoken to and try to take an interest in what is going on. Sometimes it is all right for me to go outside and play with other children or watch TV in another room, but I should always ask first. Sometimes at grown-up parties I can't find a place to put my refreshments. It's hard to just sit in a chair and try to eat from a plate and drink from a cup! But Aunt Jenny gave me some tips about this.

One thing I can do is leave room on my plate for my cup. Then I can put the plate on my lap and keep everything together. Another thing I can do is use another chair. This is a good possibility when the party is in a place where there are many folding chairs. Sometimes, if I look hard, I can even find a little table somewhere, or I can sit on the floor if it's carpeted. It's always a good idea to ask an adult before doing this, though.

The end of a grown-up party is really just like the end of any party. It's a time for friendly goodbyes and plenty of expressions of thanks. Everyone is tired but smiling, because it's been a wonderful celebration.

I just can't wait until it's party time again!

A Theme for Your Party

Parties are more fun if you plan them around a theme. You can make food and decorations to go with it—and you can even ask your guests to participate by coming in costume or bringing something to contribute to the theme. Here are some ideas for fun party themes:

> A Piggy Party (everyone wear pink)
> A Skating Costume Party
> A Mexican Christmas (with a piñata)
> An Angelic Caroling Party (with angel
>   costumes)
> On the Farm
> A Pink Valentine Party
> A Monopoly Marathon (or a Scrabble Soiree)

A Pet Party

An Olympics Party

A Pizza-Making Party (or a Bread-Baking
Party)

A Cowgirl Cookout

A Skateboard Round-up

Cowboys on the Range

Surfing at the Beach

Mountain Biking the Hills

Volunteering for the Homeless

Cleaning a Neighbor's Yard

Party on the Go

If I am attending a party at an amusement park, a pizza restaurant, or some other place outside my hosts' home, a few special
manners rules apply. For one thing, it's important to stay with
the group and not wander off. It's not very polite to make my
hosts have to hunt for me. If we are given tokens to play games,
I should keep track of my tokens and not ask for more. If an
employee of the park helps with the party, I should remember
to say thank you to her as well as to my hosts.

❯ Kid-2-Kid ❮

What Was That Strange Noise?

Boys seem to have more strange noises coming from them
than girls do. However, both boys and girls need to learn how
to handle these unexpected situations.

Believe it or not, we can and will get into many difficult situations in life. The more experiences we have in the outside world, the more unexpected situations we find ourselves in. Usually there aren't any set rules to help us know how to handle these situations. We'll look at a couple of situations that could be embarrassing and hear how to handle them with good manners.

Yawning. This is where the hand-over-mouth comes into play. If you feel a yawn coming on, the usual clenching your teeth together makes your face look distorted. Simply place your hand over your mouth and very politely say, "Oh, please excuse me, I didn't get a good night's sleep last night."

Rumbling stomach. If you can ignore it, do so. However, if those around you hear it, you might simply say, "It must be near lunch time—at least my stomach thinks so."

Hiccups. These don't rise up too often for most people, but when they do, they must be dealt with. Simply excuse yourself for a moment, go to the closest restroom, try some deep breathing, holding it as long as you can, take a drink of water, and repeat if needed. If this doesn't work, return to the group and lightly ask if anyone has a tip for getting rid of hiccups. You'll hear a bunch of ideas, I promise you.

Bad breath. Often you are the last person to know if you have bad breath. Make it a point to visit your dentist at least twice a year, brush your teeth after every meal (if possible), and floss on a regular basis. In other words, start out first with good dental health. After that, use breath mints before you meet with others. At home have a bunch of parsley in the refrigerator so you can take a clump and chew.

If someone offers you a mint, it might be a signal that your breath reflects the garlic you had earlier. Receive the mint as a gesture of kindness and don't act offended.

Sneezing. Sneezes seem to come on in the least desirable situations. However, they do give you a funny feeling in your nose first. They tell you, "Get ready, here I come!" At the first sign of that tingle, try the best you can to have your nose and mouth covered with a napkin, handkerchief, or at least your hand. Turn your head away from the crowd or away from food. After sneezing, just say, "excuse me" in an apologetic tone. Usually those around you will say back, "God bless."

Accidents at the table. Nothing is more embarrassing than knocking over a glass of water or milk at the table, particularly if you are having dinner at a social gathering or when you are a guest at someone else's home. If an accident happens at a restaurant, use a napkin to mop up until the waiter arrives to help. If you're at home, you can get some paper towels to absorb the spillage. Apologize once and don't keep talking about it.

A talker, talker, talker. We have all been trapped by talkers who have never learned to listen. They just go on and on. It's all about them. Often they never come up for air. How do I handle that person? To be honest, I don't want to listen to them all evening.

- Interrupt them occasionally with a question that might divert the conversation.

- Excuse yourself to go to the restroom.

- Excuse yourself so you can go over to a guest you must speak with.

- Have your brother, sister, or parent rescue you if he or she notes you are trapped by a talker.

- Change the subject often so at least the topic changes.

Knowing how to handle embarrassing situations when you're young will help you throughout your life. You may think problems are not good, but they teach us valuable lessons.

Kid-2-Kid

You Might Do That with Your Friends

When you get together with your friends, you probably don't open doors for each other, overuse the words *please* and *thank you*, shake hands, or take off your hat. Does that mean you're using bad manners with your friends? Not really. You and your friends understand, without really having to say anything, that some of the things you do—like pretend wrestling with each other or eating massive amounts of pizza as fast as you can or just acting goofy—are just fine when you're in each other's company. These things don't bother any of you. In fact they're fun.

However, many of the things you do with your closest pals aren't appropriate around parents, relatives, and other adults. And never do these things in public places!

Girls take a different approach to their times with friends. They usually aren't as crude as boys, but in their own ways they sometimes do things that are hurtful. So, be careful that you don't spend too long on the phone, and don't use words to demean your friends. Refuse to gossip and give wrong information. Try not to say things that will cause your girlfriend to cry.

Your Gum

There are two main things to remember about chewing gum. Don't chew it in places where you're not supposed to, like in school, at church, during meals, or anyplace where it's distracting. And don't chew it in a way that annoys other people—snapping it, talking and chewing at the same time, blowing giant bubbles that pop on your face (and *especially* any that pop on someone else's face!). When your gum's all chewed out, wrap it in paper and put it in the trash. Never stick it under a table, desk, or chair, no matter how convenient that might be!

Spitting

Unless it's a certified watermelon-seed-spitting contest, there's really no polite way to spit in public. Spitting is really gross because it usually lands on the ground where somebody steps in it. Yuck! If you have something in your mouth that you really need to spit out, find a bathroom and spit it out in the sink. And never spit on other people! This goes for girls as well as boys.

Burping

This is one area where boys make different sounds than girls. For some reason boys seem to like to burp (or make other strange sounds).

You and your friends have probably sat around trying to see who can get up the biggest, loudest, grossest burp. And you *know* that burping is bad, bad manners! So don't do it (unless you're just with your friends and you're sure they won't mind). If you accidentally do burp, just say "Excuse me," instead of, "Wow! That was a great one!"

Nose Stuff

One of the grossest things people do is pick their noses in public—and sometimes they aren't even aware of what they're doing! If you do have stuff in your nose that needs to come out pronto, head for the nearest bathroom and get it out with a tissue. Don't just dig around wherever you are and wipe it under your chair or on your sleeve! When you need to blow your nose, try not to sound like the loudest trumpet in the band. Blow into a tissue. Never wipe your nose with the back of your hand or your sleeve.

Whacky Weirdness

You know what this is all about—icky armpit sounds, inside-out eyelids, pig faces, strange voices and gestures. Once again, it's okay to do these things when you and all your friends are hanging out. But these things are definitely *not* appropriate when you're around other people.

You're with a group of kids your age and you think it's okay to start acting as crazy as you want to. You're getting a few strange looks, but hey, you're a funny guy! Pretty soon, though, nobody's paying any attention to you. Then Bradley Joe elbows you and whispers, "Hey, buddy, cut it out." Oops! You crossed that line again. How do you know when it's okay to act like a goofball and when it's not?

Check out the group you're with. If you're hanging around close friends or cousins and you guys always act this way—in fact, they expect it from you!—it's probably fine. Be careful not to get too out of control though. If people start ignoring you or giving you strange looks, cool it. And if someone tells you to stop, realize that you've crossed too far over the line and say, "Sorry." Then just calm yourself (and anyone else who followed your lead) down.

Kid-2-Kid

School Manners

Does it seem like school has so many rules? Too many? Some schools even have a big fat handbook that goes on and on about what you can and can't do. So how can you remember all these rules? Well, if you keep just a few manners in mind, knowing what to do in school will be as easy as pie—but probably not as tasty.

In the Classroom

It's really important to listen to and respect your teacher and any other adults in the school—other teachers, parent helpers, the principal, and even the custodian and lunch helpers. Follow these good manners for success in school:

- It helps everyone when you are on time—getting to class, coming back from recess, or running an errand.
- Unless you're given permission, make sure you keep your hands off other people's stuff—and especially your teachers' stuff.
- When you're taking a test, keep your eyes on your own paper. Never let other students cheat off your paper.
- It's sometimes hard not to whisper jokes to your pals or goof around a little, but try not to do it too much.

- Help out when you can, and don't worry about being called a teacher's pet. Teachers like it when you are willing to help.

At Recess Time

This is the time for you to run around the playground and spend all your extra energy. You've probably been sitting for a few hours and you have a lot of wiggles to get out. But you still do have to follow some guidelines and rules. Here's what you can do. Join in whatever game looks fun, or get a brand-new game started. Be willing to trade off playing a certain game every recess. This is a way to meet new friends too.

How many times have you heard "Me first!" on the playground? Remember that it's not that big a deal to be second or third. Join the line when you get there. It's even polite to let another student take your place if you've already had a turn. Just think, someone might do the same for you someday. Everyone should get a chance to play.

In the Lunchroom

It's tempting to start a food fight in the lunchroom with those lumpy mashed potatoes and slippery bananas. But don't do it! Don't throw anything—not even one item. It's sure to turn into a big mess, and everyone will be quick to point fingers at who started it—you!

It's okay to eat a chocolate chip cookie that your friend Weston offers you, but don't grab one out of his lunchbox. And don't swap your peanut butter sandwich for his triple sliced ham sandwich when he isn't looking. Mom spent a lot of time and effort to make you a good lunch; so be respectful and eat it all. An occasional "thank you" to Mom would be appreciated by her.

If someone else's lunch looks funny or you can't identify what it is, don't make fun of it. That is embarrassing to the other person, and it may make him not want to eat his lunch, even if he does like it. Be sure to take home what you don't eat, and put any trash where it belongs.

In the Library

The one word that librarians have wanted to hear for the last two hundred years is QUIET! Get your books and other media, ask the librarian any questions in your indoor voice. Go outside or write a note if you need to say something to your friends.

Make sure that you turn your cell phone off before you go inside the library. When you do check out books, be super careful with them. Treat them as if they were your own personal property. Use bookmarks instead of folding down the corners of pages. Be sure not to use a highlighter or make any notes in the margin of a page.

Keep pets, food, and messy little brothers or sisters away from the books. Be sure to return those books on time. Chances are someone else is eager to read them too.

School Bathrooms

Some students think it's fun to make a mess of school bathrooms by pumping large amounts of soap into the sink, stopping up the toilets, or writing on the walls. None of that is funny, and it causes extra work for the custodian. Someone has to clean up your mess.

A New Friend

Do you sometimes not know how to act when you meet a kid who is different from you, maybe someone who comes from another country or has a disability? All the other good-manners rules apply to these people (who are people just like you).

- Smile, talk, and be friendly. You shouldn't ever just ignore the other person.

- Talk to the person's inner self, not his outer self. Everybody has feelings, special needs, and special abilities. Be sure to remember that when you talk to someone who seems different. Instead of looking at a wheelchair or a skin color, try to see the real person.

- Ask if you can help. Someone from another country might appreciate help understanding our customs. Someone who is blind might need help getting around a classroom. Always ask before you help; the other person might prefer to do it herself.

Be kindly affectionate to one another with brotherly love, in honor giving preference to one another...given to hospitality.

ROMANS 12:10-13 NKJV

The Delight of Dining Etiquette

Gather Round the Table

The ideal guest is an equally ideal hostess;
the principle of both is the same; a quick sympathy,
a happy outlook, and consideration for others.

EMILY POST, *ETIQUETTE*

Using proper table manners is greatly beneficial for our home lives, but the impact of good dining etiquette reaches far beyond a meal at the family table. The home front is the training ground for your child to eventually have valuable adult life behaviors. Good table manners and social skills can mean the difference in a hiring or promotion in your career and in the future careers of your children.

Good etiquette becomes a lifestyle. You don't just put it on to impress people; you adopt proper etiquette so that it makes a lasting impression on your life and defines who you are. When you know and practice proper etiquette, it puts you at ease in all kinds of social settings, whether small gatherings or big social functions.

When you guide your children to adopt good table and eating manners, you are helping them understand how to give and receive. Each time you come to the table as a family or invite others to come to your table, you are entering a time of nourishing one another with food, conversation, and community. When guests are with you, you welcome them to this sacred time, and they become a part of the family. Breaking bread and sharing food as part of a celebration while visiting someone else's home allows you and your children to become a part of another family's traditions. Food may be one of the most constant and influential ways in which we connect to God's provision and to one another.

Your evening dinner time is a wonderful chance to practice "company" manners with your children. Mom and Dad, these manners don't all have to be taught in a single setting. Before we discuss the company manners, I want to emphasize the importance of what we call a "teachable moment" around our home. Consider Deuteronomy 6:6-7:

> These words which I command you today shall be in your heart. You shall teach them diligently to your children, and shall talk of them when you sit in your house, when you walk by the way, when you lie down, and when you rise up (NKJV).

These verses encourage us to use every opportunity to pass the values that are important to us down to the next generation. We are the primary influencers of our children. Not the neighbors, not the schools, not the media, not the church, but the people inside the four walls we call home.

Cherish your times together at the dinner table. Often it is your only time to catch up with one another after a long day of separate activities. Offer plenty of time for conversation. Intentionally slow down the pace. While you're demonstrating manners for your children, you can review the company manners needed for an upcoming evening of guests.

Make mealtime a family time whenever possible. At your table or at a restaurant, giving and receiving happens in many wonderful, relationship-building ways. Your family members learn to listen and speak graciously, offer food and accept food, and, most important, give thanks to God and receive the blessings of family and nourishment. After all, thankful people do give thanks. Here are a couple of examples:

> Come, dear Lord,
> Be our guest and become our host.
> Be pleased to bless this food
> And us who dwell here. Amen.

೨◦෨

> As we now from our bounty eat,
> Keep us humble, kind, and sweet,
> May we serve Thee, Lord, each day
> And feel Thy love, dear Lord, we pray.
>
> To God who gives us daily bread,
> A thankful song we raise,
> And pray that He who sends us food
> Will fill our hearts with praise. Amen.

Manners School Family Activity:
Setting a Table 101

Let's first look at how to set a table and then how to use the table setting properly. If you know the road map, you won't be surprised or awkward when you begin dining. If you are ever in doubt, watch what the hosts do and follow their actions. If you're the host, these next sections will be very helpful to you.

The Silver Setting

An easy way to remember which utensil to use is to work your way toward the center from both sides.

Formal Dinner

A. napkin

B. service plate

C. soup bowl on a liner plate

D. bread and butter plate with butter knife

E. water glass

F. red wine glass

G. white wine glass

H. fish fork

I. dinner fork

J. salad fork

K. dessert fork

L. knife

M. fish knife

N. teaspoon

O. soup spoon

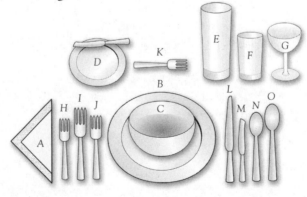

The Silver Setting

An easy way to remember which utensil to use is to work your way in on both sides.

Luncheon

A. napkin

B. luncheon plate

C. soup (or other first course plate) on a liner plate

D. bread and butter plate with butter knife

E. water glass

F. wine glass

G. luncheon fork

H. knife

I. teaspoon

J. soup spoon

Silverware

The proper placement of your silverware signals to the server at what stage of the meal you are. If you pause for a breather, place the utensils in the resting position. This signals that you aren't finished yet and that you plan to continue your meal.

Resting Position

When you are finished with a meal, place your utensils at the four o'clock position. It tells your server that you're finished and that he can remove your plate from the table.

Finished Position

Manners at Mealtime

Have you ever wondered why there are so many table-manners rules?

I have. So I asked my Aunt Jenny why it's so important to do things like keep our elbows off the table and chew with our mouths closed.

She said we need table manners because mealtime is so important. It's when we feed our bodies with food. It's also when we feed our spirits with love and friendship. And it's easiest to do that when meals are peaceful and happy.

That's what table manners are really for—keeping mealtime enjoyable for everyone.

Preparing for the Meal

Take time to learn what a basic table setting looks like and how you are to use the utensils properly. Most of the time, things are kept pretty simple at home, right? In fact, at our house things are very casual, but we still remember to use table manners. I sometimes have to remind my mom about some of the manners! I figure that a family is always in training!

Of course, sometimes place settings get a lot *fancier*, like the example given in this chapter's family activity. When a setting is more formal, there is a separate salad plate and a bread-and-butter plate. Besides a water glass, there are sometimes glasses for other beverages, or cups for tea or coffee. Sometimes there are three forks and two spoons. But the same basic rules still apply—dinner plate in the center, forks and napkins left, knives and spoons right, drinks right, plus extra plates go on the left.

Knowing these rules helps me when I go to a restaurant or somebody's house and I don't know what to do with part of my place setting. The main rule to remember is that the things you use first are on the outside, farthest from the plate. That means the napkin is farthest left because you pick it up first, then a little fork for salad, and finally the dinner fork. On the right, the soup spoon is farthest right, then the teaspoon and the knife.

If I'm not sure what to do, I just watch the people around me and do what they do.

Before Dinner Is Served

The first thing I do at dinnertime happens before I actually come to the table—I wash my hands! Then I go to the dinner table and wait for everybody else to come so we can sit down together. At home I always know where my place is. If I'm visiting, I wait for my hostess or host to tell me where to sit—or I look for a place card with my name on it. Then I wait for the hostess to sit down before I do.

In our family, we always say a blessing—a short thank-you prayer. We hold hands and take turns saying it. My friend Yolanda's family calls it "saying grace," and her father usually does it. My friend Jessica's family doesn't say grace at all, but she always bows her head politely with us when she eats over at my house. (When I'm at her house, I like to say a quiet little thank-you prayer inside my head before we start.)

Then I pick up my napkin and place it in my lap. (I never flap it open or tuck it in my shirt like a bib.) If it's a big dinner napkin, I leave it folded in half, with the fold toward me.

Making Mealtimes Pleasant

Mealtimes are nicest when everyone starts and finishes at about the same time. So I wait for the hostess (or my mom) to start before I do, and I try to eat at about the same pace as everybody else.

How I sit at the table can make a difference in how pleasant a meal is for me and others. I try not to rock my chair or move around too much—that's distracting to others and might cause spills. And I try to sit up straight with my elbows at my side (not on the table) and my hands in my lap when I'm not using them. This looks nicer, helps food go down better, and even helps keep my clothes clean.

Pleasant conversation is also an important part of mealtime—as important as eating. But conversation and eating shouldn't happen at the very same second! If I chew first, swallow, and then talk, people won't have to look at a yucky mouthful of chewed food. (I try to chew with my mouth closed.) All this is easier if I remember to take small bites and sips instead of big gulps and forkfuls. And I should never wave a fork or a piece of carrot around in my hand while I talk.

Another way to keep mealtimes pleasant for everyone is to eat quietly (without chomps and slurps) and to remember to use polite language.

What If I Don't Like It?

We all have certain foods we don't like. I can't stand broccoli. My friend Donna doesn't like meat loaf. Jessica is allergic to milk and milk products.

So what do we do if we go over to Yoli's house for dinner and find ourselves looking at bowls of meat loaf, broccoli with cheese sauce, and mashed potatoes?

What we shouldn't do is look at the food on the table, make a face, and say, "Yuck" or "I can't eat that."

There are lots of better ways to handle the situation.

We can simply say "No, thank you" when the food is offered. Even better, we can say, "Just a little, please," or just take a very small serving from the bowl. Then we can eat just a few bites.

What if you're allergic to something and *can't* eat it? My friend Barbara, who is very allergic to peanuts, quietly lets the hostess know. And if she can, Barbara explains about her allergy before she goes over to eat.

What to Do with a Knife and Fork

There's a polite way to eat almost any food. We eat most foods, of course, with a fork. In America, we hold forks and spoons like pencils, scooping our food onto the utensils.

If I'm served soup, I tip the spoon away from me, scoop up a little soup, and sip it from the side of the spoon. It's all right to tilt the bowl away from me to get the last of the soup, but I shouldn't pick up the bowl and drink from it. And I should never, ever slurp!

Bread goes on the bread-and-butter plate if there is one, or just on the side of the plate. When the butter is passed, I put a little bit on my plate and use it to butter pieces of bread as I eat them. I shouldn't butter my bread all at once. It's better to break off a small piece, butter it, and then eat it.

The same thing goes for meat. Instead of cutting it all up into little pieces first, I cut off each piece before I eat it.

Sometimes salad comes in big pieces that are messy to put in my mouth. Aunt Jenny said it's okay to cut the lettuce into smaller pieces with a knife and fork.

It's all right to eat some foods with your fingers: grapes, plums, cherries, celery, carrot sticks, pickles, olives, radishes, corn on the cob, crab and lobster claws, artichokes, and dry, crisp bacon. (Be sure and clean your fingers with a napkin afterward.) Later we'll look at other kinds of foods and how to eat them.

Once I've picked up a knife, fork, or spoon, it should never go back on the table. When I'm not using it, it should rest on the edge of my plate—the whole thing, not just the eating part. Soup spoons should be left in the bowl or on the plate that comes under the bowl.

If Something Happens

Mealtimes don't always go smoothly. Sometimes I spill something or get something stuck in my mouth or even make an embarrassing sound. Aunt Jenny says the best thing to do with situations like these is to take care of them quietly. If I knock over my glass, I just say "I'm sorry" and help clean up the mess. If I burp or my stomach growls, I just say a quiet "Excuse me" and go on with my meal.

What if something ends up in my mouth that I don't want— like a bone or a piece of gristle or something that's too hot or tastes really awful? It's never polite to just spit it out.

If it's too hot, I can take a drink of water. If it tastes bad, I should swallow it quickly and take a bite of something else. If it's something I can't swallow, I can remove it with my fingertips or the tip of my fork and place it on the side of my plate.

If I have something stuck between my teeth or some other problem I can't take care of pleasantly at the table, I ask to be excused and then take the problem to another room. (When I leave in the middle of a meal, I should leave my napkin on my chair.)

Finishing Up

I always feel good when I've finished a nice meal. My tummy is satisfied, and I've had a nice time talking to my family and friends. What do I do then?

First, I wait for everyone else to finish—or at home I may ask politely to be excused. Then I place my knife, fork, and spoon side by side in the middle of my plate with the tines of the fork pointing down. I place my napkin loosely (not folded) beside my plate, and I push back my chair carefully.

It's nice to offer to help clean up. (At home I always help.) But no matter what else I do, there's one important part of table manners I should never forget. That is saying "Thank you very much" to the one who made the meal.

Fast-Food Manners

Mealtime manners are for everywhere—even in a burger or taco place. Fast-food restaurants even call for some special kinds of manners. It's important to be courteous to the person who takes my order. It's also good to think ahead about what I want so I won't hold up the line while I try to decide what to order. I shouldn't take more napkins, straws, or condiments (ketchup, mustard, relish) than I need, and, of course, I should use good manners while I'm eating. (Chewing with my mouth open is just as disgusting in a Burger Palace as it is at home.) Finally, I should throw away my trash when I am through and leave my table clean for the next people who eat there.

The heart of mealtime manners is to act so that everyone at the table, or in the booth, or in the car, including you, can enjoy the food and the company—even when you're eating on the run.

Getting Specific: Table Manners

Table manners change a bit when the food isn't served as a sit-down meal. But it's pretty easy to adapt your manners to suit the situation. Each time you do this, you will become more and more comfortable using your dashing dining skills!

If the food is served family style, I pick up the dish nearest me and offer it to the person on my right. When a dish is passed to me, I put some of the food on my plate, return the serving spoon to the dish, and pass it to the person on my right. I try to pay attention to how much food there is and how many people are at the table—I don't want to take so much that somebody doesn't get enough. I don't pick through the dish to find the best piece. I just take what is nearest to me. And if I am asked to pass a glass or a cup, I only touch the outside, not the rim.

Sometimes food is served buffet style, which means I go to a different table and serve myself from a lot of different dishes. The most important thing to remember about serving myself at a buffet is not to put too much on my plate. It's better to start with small amounts and go back to the buffet table if I want seconds. I also need to remember not to touch anything that is not actually going on my plate and not to take too much of one dish.

Proper Seating

Depending on the mix of the gathering, the host is seated at one end of the table and the hostess at the other end. A male honored guest sits to the right of the hostess, and if the honored guest is a female, she is seated to the right of the host. Balance the rest of the guests male, female, male, female.

Table Courtesies

Always watch what the host does. Wait for the hostess to be seated before you sit down. In some settings, someone may offer a prayer of thanksgiving Then wait for the host to indicate in word or by action that it's okay to begin eating.

A Course on Courses

The number of courses offered depends on how formal the dinner is. Most dinners will include five courses.

1. The appetizer or hors d'oeuvre. This might be as simple as nuts or cheese and crackers served in the living room before dinner.
2. Soup
3. Salad
4. Entrée. This is the main course. It will consist of meat, fish, pasta, or poultry with vegetables and a starch, such as rice or potatoes.
5. Dessert

The Napkin

Watch the host to see when you should unfold your napkin. As soon as the host does so, that is a signal for you to do likewise. Here are a couple of reminders regarding the placement and use of the napkin whether you are the host or the guest.

• Unfold the napkin to the half-folded position and place in your lap with the centerfold against your waistline.

- If you leave the table during the meal, leave your napkin on the seat of the chair. This signals to the server that you'll be returning.
- Placing your napkin to the right of your plate indicates that you're finished with your meal. The napkin need not be folded.
- Blot your mouth after drinking and eating during the meal.

When to Leave the Table

Watch for the host to stand and suggest the guests go to the living room, where more coffee and tea may be served.

Mom, Can I Use My Fingers?

Did you know that certain foods are meant to be eaten in certain ways? It's okay to eat some foods with your fingers. You just need to clean your fingers with a napkin afterward. Sometimes it depends on where you're eating the food. If you have fried chicken at a picnic, you almost always use your fingers. In fact, I think it makes it tastier to eat it this way! But if you have a nice piece of chicken at a fancy restaurant, then the fork and knife will be used. It will still be delicious, I promise.

Again, if you're at someone else's house, watch the hostess to see how she eats the item. Many times the hostess will inform you that it's okay to use your fingers.

This is an extensive list of foods that can be tricky to determine how to eat properly. You might never have eaten some of these foods! Go through this list with your family. When you run across a food you've never eaten before, talk about trying it together as a family sometime soon!

Artichokes. Many people have never tried this wonderful vegetable. Each leaf is pulled off, dipped into your favorite sauce, and then pulled quietly and delicately through your front teeth to remove the soft, delicious portion of the leaf. You'll need to have an extra plate or bowl handy to discard the uneaten part of the leaves. Next, take a knife or fork to scrape the prickly part off so that the heart can be eaten. Never scrape with your fingers. That's a no-no!

Asparagus. If this vegetable is not cooked, you may pick up the stem with your fingers and eat it. However, if it is cooked and soggy or served with a sauce, you would cut it into bite-size pieces and eat it with a fork.

Bagels, cream cheese, and lox. This combination is ideal as a finger food. Most delis will serve the various parts separately, and you put them together to form an open-faced sandwich. To do this, you'll use a knife to spread the cream cheese and a fork to lift the lox and onions into place.

Breads. There's no set rule on how to approach this food item; it all depends on what type of bread you're eating. A normal slice of bread, roll, or muffin may be torn into small pieces (two or three bites at a time). These are buttered and eaten before you tear off another two or three bites.

English muffins and bagels may be broken in half and made into half-sandwich form. If they're too tough, a knife is permissible to cut the pieces into halves. The rule is to break the bread if the fiber of the bread is breakable or cut it if the fiber needs a knife in order to portion it into bite-size pieces.

Candy and nuts. The bowl will have a small spoon for you to use to scoop the candy or nuts from the serving dish to your hand. Whatever your fingers touch is yours. Don't put candy or nuts back into the bowl.

Chicken. Southerners, by tradition, usually consider fried chicken a finger food and by heritage will automatically eat with their fingers.

Corn on the cob. This food item is usually served at a very informal meal. You can eat the corn holding the cob ends with your hands or with cob skewers. Take special care to not sound like a pig as you munch the corn. A kernel of corn will likely get stuck in a space between two of your teeth. Since toothpicks aren't served at the table, excuse yourself politely from the table and go to the restroom to remove the stuck corn.

Desserts. What sweet-toothed guest has ever turned down a refreshing dessert? There are various sizes and shapes of dessert forks and spoons, but most of us don't have these in our kitchen drawer. Cakes and pies are served with a normal fork; custards and ice cream need a regular spoon. This way the sides and the bottom of the cup can be scraped clean. We don't want to leave any morsel!

Dips. The rule for dipping chips, crackers, or vegetables is that you only get one dip into the sauce or dressing. No double dipping allowed. Be sure to have a big stack of napkins alongside the dip bowl for your guests to wipe their fingers and mouths.

Finger foods. Chips, cookies, candy, pretzels, hard-boiled eggs, popcorn, etc., may always be eaten by hand.

Fondue. If you've never tried a fondue dinner or dessert, you should try it. It is great fun. You'll want your parents to set it up and be there with you because the oil that is used to cook the food is very hot. The chocolate used for dipping dessert items is also very hot in the fondue pot. Hot and yummy! When your food item in the fondue pot is cooked (or coated with chocolate), remove it from the long fondue fork with a dinner fork. Place the food on your plate. Be careful not to drip on the tablecloth.

Fruits, whole. It is okay to eat fruit whole if you are outdoors, but if at a meal, you will use a different method.

- One, pierce the fruit with a fork and cut the side off with your knife, away from the fruit's pit.
- Two, cut the piece into bite-size sections.
- Three, eat each section with your fork.

Melons are eaten with a spoon. Scissors are good to cut off clusters of grapes. If you don't have scissors, plucking off individual grapes is okay. Take the seeds from your mouth carefully and place on a corner of your plate.

Fish. Be careful when eating fish that the bones don't get into your mouth—and even worse—into your throat. Pick the bones out of the fish (with a fork) before you put any fish into your mouth, and if you missed one, discreetly remove it from your mouth with your fingers. Place bones to the side of your dinner plate.

Gravies and sauces. Often we add these to our entrée to give it a special flavor or appearance. If a sauce spoon is not available, it is okay to scoop gravy or sauce with a regular dinner spoon.

Gum. Chewing gum is off limits at the dining room table. Dispose of it before you're seated. Be sure to wrap the gum in paper or tissue before throwing it away in the host's wastebasket.

Olives. These favorites can be served by themselves or mixed with other foods. If they're served separately or on a vegetable tray, they would be considered finger food (it's best to serve those that have no pits). If they appear in a salad, you can pierce them with your salad fork and eat them.

Onion rings. If these delicious offerings are served in a fast-food restaurant, they're finger food. Be sure to use a napkin to wipe your fingers and mouth. If you encounter them in a nice restaurant, they are likely served atop a fine piece of beef. In this case you would cut them into bite-size pieces and eat them with a fork.

Pizza. This leading fast food is enjoyed by young and old. If you lack coordination in getting the pizza from the serving tray to your mouth, you may want to take a piece, put it on your plate, cut it into small pieces, and use a fork. If you're somewhat coordinated and can risk bringing crust, topping, and stringy cheese to your mouth, try the finger-food method.

Potatoes, baked. The easiest way is to use your fingers to split the potato (be careful, it's hot) and a fork to mash the sour cream or butter into it.

Salads. Vegetables are a vital part of a well-balanced diet. When serving a salad as one of your courses, you have one of two options in how it is prepared and served. If you are tearing the lettuce into small pieces and mixing it with bite-size vegetables, this salad can be eaten with just a fork. If you're using large pieces of lettuce, be sure to provide a proper knife and fork so your guests can cut the larger pieces into more manageable bite-size pieces. If you are the guest and no knife is provided, use the side of your fork to cut the lettuce leaves into smaller pieces for easier eating.

Sandwiches. There are many kinds of sandwiches and sandwich-like foods. Some favorites are club, pita, tacos, hot dogs, and sloppy joes. Eat them as finger food, paying close attention to the ketchup, mustard, relish, and hot sauce. Watch that these condiments don't fall out and drip on your new shirt. Have a bunch of paper napkins nearby.

Sometimes the fillings spill out over the bread, shell, or bun and fall back to the plate. The tasty morsels (often this is the best part of a sandwich) that fall to the plate can be eaten by using a fork.

Shish-kabob. Remove the elements from the stick onto the plate, pulling the food off with a fork. Some people barbeque lots of meat and veggies and even fruit using kabobs. They are quite delicious.

Shrimp. It's okay to use your fingers when you're served shrimp in their shell. However, if the shrimp have already been peeled, cut them with a knife and eat with a fork.

Soup. Fill the soup spoon with the liquid and draw it away from the bowl before it's redirected to your mouth. In formal settings, several different spoons may be used when serving or being served soup:

- large oval spoon for clear soups
- large round spoon for cream soups
- small round spoon for broths
- porcelain spoon for Chinese soups
- lacquer soup bowl with Japanese bowl (which may be lifted to the mouth for direct drinking of the soup)

Whichever spoon and soup you're eating, you may not slurp. When finished with the soup, you may leave the spoon in the bowl or rest it on the soup plate.

Spaghetti. Lots of people think you are supposed to twirl pasta against a spoon—but that's not true, not even in Italy. The pasta is to be twirled on the fork against the plate until it makes a tight ball so that it can be raised to your mouth easily. Make sure the sauce doesn't drip on your clothes. Ask for a bib if you want to be extra careful.

Steak. Provide the proper steak knife so you can cut the meat into bite-size pieces.

Sushi and sashimi. On the West Coast you will find almost as many sushi bars as you will Starbucks coffee cafes. Every block and every strip mall seems to have at least one restaurant that specializes in sushi. Sushi is lifted clear from the serving plate with chopsticks, dipped into the soy sauce with green horseradish mixed in, and then lifted to the mouth. It is usually eaten in one huge bite. Sashimi can be eaten with chopsticks or a fork.

Tomatoes. These are so messy that if you aren't careful, the juice can get all over your outfit and leave stains. Put a whole cherry tomato into your mouth and clamp down on it with lips firmly closed. Make sure nothing squirts out of the corner of your mouth. If you need to cut up your larger tomatoes into more manageable bite-size pieces, use the side of your fork.

Vegetables. Cooked vegetables seem to slip around the plate when you try to catch them with a fork. Raw vegetables are so crisp that you're afraid everyone can hear you chew. It's okay to use a piece of bread or a knife blade as a pusher, and be sensitive that raw vegetables can make a lot of noise. But you're usually not as loud as you think.

Go International

More and more families are traveling outside of America. Have you been fortunate enough to travel to another country? Or even to another part of America that favors a unique style of cooking? It can be quite challenging to adjust to different food selections and cooking styles unless you are a little prepared in advance. If you live in a fairly large city, you'll find a lot of ethnic foods and may get to like different cuisines. Even smaller towns these days often have a more global choice of restaurants.

Help your mom and dad expand their eating horizons. You can encourage the idea of choosing ethnic restaurants in your area that serve foods you don't typically eat at home. Make it a fun night by studying up on that restaurant's culture and dining practices so you can share facts and fun details with your family while you are eating out. It is fun to discover and appreciate the different customs, preferences, and flavors that children from other cultures enjoy. And you'll help your family discover some new favorite dishes along the way.

> Kid-2-Kid

Dining Tips Summary

We've gone over settings and situations that you might not face until you are a lot older. I mean, how often do we hang with friends who eat with a separate salad fork (or who eat salad)? But later on in life, you'll be glad that you and your family decided to explore these tips and facts. You'll be the comfortable one at a fancy school event or a community fund raiser. Maybe you'll attend a scholarship or awards ceremony that includes a formal meal. How cool is it that you'll know what to do and you can give your friends pointers throughout the meal.

It's a lot to take in, so let's close this section with a dining-manners quick-tips summary. Consider it your parent-approved cheat sheet for manners. It'd also be kinda fun to create your own list of quick tips to post in your kitchen or to have handy for a read through before you go to the fanciest restaurant in town because your visiting Uncle Lou wants oysters and caviar. It could happen! Aren't you glad you'll be prepared?

Dining Manners Quick Tips
(Your Cheat Sheet to Proper Dining)

- The gentlemen are to pull out the chairs for the ladies and help them to be seated.

- The napkin is put on your lap with folded side toward your waist.

- Watch the hostess to see what to do next.

- The honored guest is the first to be served, and the lady to the left is served next.

- "As the ships sail out to sea, I spoon my soup away from me."

- When you are asked to pass the salt, pass the pepper too.

- Avoid placing your elbows on the table, and never hunch over and "hug" your plate.

- Food should always be passed to the right (counter-clockwise).

- Leaving food on your plate is not good manners.

- Cutting up your salad into bite-size pieces is up to you.

- Serving dishes are passed around the table until all have been served. The host is the last to be served.

- Any dirty utensil should go beside the plate—soup spoons can be left in the soup bowl.

- You are permitted to use your fingers to pick up bread. Cut or tear off a small piece of bread before breaking off more. Butter each small piece of bread as you tear it off.

- The bread plate is placed to the left of the dinner plate.

- Have servings of butter, salt, and pepper at each end of the table for ease of passing.

- If you must leave the table after being seated, excuse yourself and place your napkin on your chair.

- Never hurry your meal—these are important times together with your family or friends.

Direct your children onto the right path,
and when they are older, they will not leave it.

PROVERBS 22:6 NLT

The Comfort of Confidence at All Times

Building Confidence Muscles

If you doubt you can accomplish something,
then you can't accomplish it.
You have to have confidence in your ability,
and then be tough enough to follow through.

ROSALYNN CARTER

Teaching manners to children can seem, to some, to be about rules and propriety, but not about daily living. There might be parents who think you are extreme to make manners a part of your family tradition of teaching, training, and growing your children. These are usually the same parents who assume their kids will just pick up on social cues and appropriate behavior in school or by being in social settings. We all know how well that usually turns out! The secret they have missed out on is that manners are less about rules and more about passing on incredible life skills and lessons to your children. Your kids are blessed to be receiving the gifts of wisdom, kindness, insight, truth, and one of the most life-influencing gifts: confidence.

Manners build confidence muscles.

Each time your children use their learned manners at home, church, school, or out in the community, they are strengthening those confidence muscles. Children who are given encouragement to practice those manners are being encouraged to step out of their shell, to see beyond their worries, and to extend courtesies that connect them to other people. It is a wonderful moment when you witness your child, especially a timid child, express his thoughts or offer up kind words to a peer, a neighbor, a relative, or even a person he has just met in a social situation.

When you provide your child with examples of social manners, you are showing her a way to be comfortable in all kinds of situations, even the unexpected ones. Children with good manners are easy to single out when you gather a group of kids together. They are excellent leaders, mediators, encouragers, and teammates. They more readily understand instruction than many of the others, and they grasp the importance of serving the group over just serving themselves. Your well-mannered kids will still want to be chosen first for fun activities or praised for their excellent scores. They'll want the purple candy instead of the green one they received. There will be times when they are tired and crabby and stubborn. After all, they're kids, and they are never perfect. But as they grow and learn to make decisions, those confidence muscles will give them strength to be and do their very best.

A confident child grows into a confident adult—one who knows how to interact in most social and business situations and has the ability to communicate with others even when faced with demanding or difficult circumstances. In other words, confidence enables grace to prevail under pressure.

As you or your children read aloud the Kid-2-Kid sections about confidence, discuss ways that each of you can build those confidence muscles. Be honest about your own learning curve and struggles so that your family members will be all the more comfortable sharing about their worries or insecurities. And remember that each child's natural areas of confidence will differ from your own and from other kids' their age. Some children have no trouble talking to adults, but when they are with their peers, they shy away from communication or leadership. Other children might achieve high marks in the classroom but be very afraid to try anything outside of that safe zone. In this section, you and your kids will learn a lot about one another and about how to encourage one another.

We're each made so wonderfully unique. Reinforce that message over and over to your children. When they begin to believe that God made them to be so very special, their confidence muscles will flex with faith!

Manners School Family Activity: Camp Confidence

Confidence is not developed overnight. As adults, we *still* struggle to be confident or competent in certain areas. For many moms and dads, parenting triggers their biggest uncertainties and insecurities. So this section will be a great one for every family member.

The family activity for developing confidence through manners is a bit different from the other family activity sections. To build confidence, you need time, effort, and, ideally, new challenges and settings. Consider this an ongoing activity for your family, and commit to using everyday activities and new situations to build the confidence muscles in your kids and in yourselves. Muscles of the physical kind as well as the confidence kind need to be consistently used, stretched, and challenged in order to be their most effective. And everybody's "workout" plan won't be the same because we all need to build up different areas for different reasons. So let's get started by examining who needs what.

Talking is the best place to start. Gather the family together and discuss which settings, situations, and challenges bring out a lack of confidence and which ones bring out a strong sense of confidence. Read through the following with your family and have everyone share. Skip or revise those steps that aren't age appropriate. If you have a little one who has never gone into a store alone to buy her own piece of candy, you could present it as, "When you do these things someday, how do you think you'll feel," or go on to the next line.

Ask each family member to use these numbers/descriptions to describe how they feel when they are in the settings or situations listed below:

1. I feel strong and highly confident

2. I feel confident in my ability but not comfortable in the setting or with myself

3. I feel unsure of what to do or how to act; not confident at all

- _____ Order food at a restaurant or purchase an item at a store

- _____ Walk into a room full of people (a cafeteria at school, a school or church class, your own living room when there is a gathering of your parents' or sibling's friends)

- _____ Am asked to try something new at home, at school, in sports activities

- _____ Need to speak in front of others

- _____ Need to speak one-on-one with someone I don't know well

- _____ Ask for help from someone I don't know

- _____ Ask for help from someone I do know

- _____ Can't figure out how to do something on my own

- _____ Wait alone in a public place for Mom or Dad

- _____ Go into a store or place of service alone

- _____ Read aloud or present my ideas to others

- _____ Help with chores or activities at home or at school

- _____ Have to lead an activity

- _____ Ask to play with someone or participate in their activity

- _____ Ask someone to join me to play or to do an activity

- _____ Need to make a decision about where to go or what to do next

- _____ Need to make a choice in front of friends

- _____ Am put down or made fun of by a peer

- _____ Stay over at a friend's home

- _____ Stay as a guest of someone I don't know well

- _____ Make a mistake in front of others

- _____ Attend a social gathering of mostly adults (picnic, class, concert, party, etc.)

- _____ Attend a social gathering of mostly kids (party, class, field trip, event, etc.)

- _____ Think about my future

Write in situations that you know directly impact your child or yourself. This will allow for more specific conversations.

- _____

- _____

- _____

- _____

- _____

- _____

Were there any surprises? Have you shared about your areas of insecurity as well? Do you have examples from your own childhood about overcoming insecurities? Share that with your kids. Create an open dialogue with your children so they can come to you when they aren't feeling sure of themselves, their abilities, or the situations they find themselves in. Sometimes a child is in a situation he shouldn't be in, so his discomfort is also a vital thing for him to listen to and follow. By exploring what confidence is and how manners and skills can help your children accomplish the above actions with ease, you also help them discern when their discomfort is about a serious threat or worry…one that should be met with caution. Knowing the difference will empower your kids to make their way in the world first as confident and caring children and then as confident and caring adults.

Personalized Field Trips

Life is one big classroom, isn't it? We're fortunate to be able to participate in learning every day and in every circumstance. If you share an attitude of enthusiasm with your kids, they will see new situations and challenges, big or small, as opportunities. It isn't about being the best or reaching levels of achievement. Those might be the fruit of a child's growing confidence, but instilling manners is about transforming the heart and encouraging goodness while building the strength to make wise decisions and to follow those decisions with wise and compassionate actions.

The most common challenge to a child's confidence is participating in a social gathering. Whether she is the guest or the host, among friends or surrounded by strangers, around adults or hanging out with peers, in a person's home or in a public place… a child will face insecurities.

Thank goodness for manners. And what good are manners if they go unused? Get ready to plan a few confidence-camp adventures for your family. Your assessment of areas of insecurity will show you exactly where to go and what to do. If your child is timid about doing something new that involves interacting with a professional or a customer-service person, select this as an activity. Maybe your seven-year-old has not checked out a library book on his own. Perfect. Plan a Saturday morning to do just that. This way your child experiences something that might be intimidating if he were alone, but now it becomes an adventure that you are doing together.

When you plan for this Saturday morning, discuss how manners will make a difference. Return to role-playing if that is effective with this child. Have him practice politely asking for help, asking for more information, and inquiring whether he needs to do anything else before he leaves the library. Reinforce how using "please" and "thank you" is not only polite but becomes a way to have a friendly exchange with someone he doesn't know… like the librarian. Always encourage your child to be himself. If he wants to say he is excited to read the book he's checking out, then he should share that with the librarian. When you go to the library, be sure your child knows where you are, but you don't need to stay right by him. He'll grow to understand that communication with people is about connecting with people, not just getting one's way or getting something done.

Decide what is best for each individual child and the confidence-camp adventure you've chosen for each one. For little ones, you might want to be right there, but refrain from doing the talking for the child. That's a great first step. We know that our kids can use their voices. Oh my, do we know! We hear them throughout the day and especially when we want silence or it's time for bed. But using that voice to present a need or thought to a stranger becomes a challenge. Children who learn to ask questions and express concerns and opinions within the safety of their parents' support will blossom. It's wonderful to see that happen as a child grows in confidence.

The library is one example of an outing. The options are limitless. A restaurant is a great place to have your child practice using polite language to make requests. She will learn to use the same manners and courtesies whether at a fast-food counter or a more formal dining establishment. Your company picnic is an ideal place to encourage your more timid child to interact with adults by politely asking people's names and sharing about something of interest to her in conversation. Again, role-playing beforehand is an excellent tool.

For the child who is afraid to try new things, the confidence adventures can be numerous. Don't push so hard that it becomes a fearful experience. If your child doesn't like to try something new and your first activity is to go rock climbing, you could lose some trust. However, if you choose an activity that you know interests him on a personal level, he will experience the rewards of attempting something different. If you have a young daughter who loves to read about space and science, your activity might be to attend a class about building model rockets. A class requires a child to ask questions, clarify instructions, and expand her comfort zone a little by learning in a new setting.

You will have fun coming up with ways to boost your child's confidence. This also becomes a chance for your family to try new things together. Along the way, pay attention to what your child is sharing about his confidence level. Determine together which manners make each adventure more successful and enjoyable— strong communication, kind interaction, thoughtful decision making, thinking of others' feelings, inviting others to participate, sharing information and supplies, listening well, etc.

Camp confidence lasts a lifetime and becomes a way to view the challenges, obstacles, and opportunities along the journey.

Lead the Way

Leaders are really important! They're the ones other people follow and look up to. They get chosen to do a lot of great things. People speak highly of (say a lot of good things about) them. And just about everyone wants to be their friend. So can good manners help you to become a good leader? Of course they can! And even though you're still a kid, you can become a leader in many places—at school, at summer camp, on a team, in the neighborhood, with your brothers and sisters. Let's learn about what it takes to lead!

Off to a Great Start

It's easier to lead if you stay away from problems in the first place. When you're upset about something, your best bet is to do something positive. So if that mean sixth-grader has been on your case again, don't fight him or spread rumors about him. If your little brother is still being a pest, resist the urge to show off your new karate moves on him. Think *positive*. Go for a bike ride. Talk to someone about the problem. Run around the block.

You can also try to stop problems before they happen. How do you do this? Tell the truth. Keep your promises. Choose your friends wisely. Stay away from the wrong crowd. Avoid places where kids tend to get into trouble. Get involved in some good activities.

Oh, Brother! (Oh, Sister!)

Brothers and sisters don't always get along with each other, do they? However, did you know that you can be friends with your siblings? Despite your differences, you actually have a lot in common with them—like your parents, the house or apartment you live in, things your family likes to do, memories you share—and having stuff in common usually makes for great friendships! Sure, you're going to have your tiffs. We all do. But there are some ways to make sure you fight less and play more. Share your stuff. Respect their things. Play their games sometimes. And try your best to solve problems without hitting or screaming. You can be a leader in your own family.

Remember that when you are indoors, you use your indoor voice. Save your loud voice for when you are outside. The Golden Rule also applies to brothers and sisters.

Be a Diplomat

Do you know what a diplomat is? A diplomat is a person who gets along well with just about everyone. If you'd like to be a diplomat, do your best to be nice to each person you see throughout the day, even your friend's bratty little sister. This is actually pretty easy to do if you look for the good points in people. Most of us have at least a few (even that little sister)! Diplomats also have very good judgment, which means they usually say or do the *right* thing. (That's because they think about it first.) They don't call kids mean names—even in fun—and never tease others in a cruel way. They also stay in control even when everyone else isn't. Everyone likes to have a diplomat around!

Being a diplomat means you are a peacekeeper. Keep your voice calm when those around you are using loud voices. Diplomats don't take sides. They are able to remain neutral at all times.

"I Goofed!"

Leaders aren't perfect. Sometimes they do mess up. And

chances are you will too...someday! So when you're wrong, admit it. Say "I'm sorry" to the person you hurt. Don't blame someone else for your mistake, even if that would be a really easy way out. Be honest; think about how others feel, and learn something from what you did wrong. If you're like most of us, you probably will make a lot of mistakes in life, but you're doing a great job if you are able to keep from making the same mistake twice.

When There's Conflict

Life is awesome! You're a great leader; you're almost always doing the right thing, and then *wham!* You run into Bruce the Bully, and suddenly everything goes down the drain.

Now what do you do? The main thing is to keep yourself in control. Be smart enough to walk away from a bad situation. Or take a friend along and try talking to Bruce if things are still going poorly. If the situation gets out of hand, ask an adult for help—especially if Bruce starts threatening people and you think he's serious about it. Don't be afraid to report any scary or dangerous words or actions to someone in charge, even if you're worried about being called a tattletale. It's important to keep everyone safe, and reporting behavior that gives you the creeps is the *bravest* thing you can do.

Confidence When Away from Home

Places to go and people to see! Think of all the places you go in a week—school, church, your friend's house. Now think of all the places you go in a year—sporting events, family vacations, field trips, movies, restaurants. You really get out! When you're out and about, don't forget to bring along your manners. All the same manners that you've learned so far apply in public places—those places where you're with a lot of other people.

That Hat

You're never separated from your favorite hat. From the time you get up in the morning to the time you go to bed, that hat is on your head. But is it okay to wear that hat no matter where you are? Sorry, it's not. It is good manners to wear your hat outside. That's what hats were made for—to protect you from rain, wind, and sun. But take it off during the national anthem at a sporting event or to say the Pledge of Allegiance. Also take it off during meals. You see lots of guys (even adults) wearing their hats indoors these days. Does that make it good manners? Not really. It's best to leave the hat off, especially in a church or synagogue or at a formal event. And if your mom or another grown-up tells you to take off that hat, take it off, even if you have "hat hair" underneath!

These guidelines are appropriate not only for boys but also for girls. Hats have become such a big "fashion statement," but manners come first.

Sporting Events

Besides the no-hat-during-anthem rule, keep in mind a few more manners when you're at a sporting event. First of all, remember to practice your "good fan" manners. During the national anthem, stand quietly at attention and put your hand over your heart. (It's your right hand.) Save your whoops and yells until *after* the singer has finished. When you're leaving the stadium and it's super crowded, go with the flow. Don't try to push and shove your way through. At best, you'll get separated from the group you're with. At worse, you'll make some three-hundred-pound weightlifter in the crowd very, very upset.

It's wise to have a designated spot to meet if you happen to get separated. We used to tell our children when they were young to "just hug the tree" (meaning don't wander off, but let Mom and Dad find you rather than have you leave your "lost spot" to find them). Given time, they will find you.

Crunch-Munch, Sip-Slurp

You're at the Smithsonian, looking at all the cool exhibits in the National Air and Space Museum. You're also *super* hungry. That can of Coke and Snickers bar in your backpack would sure hit the spot right now. So do you whip them out then and there for a midafternoon snack? Not if you want to see the rest of the exhibits! Food and drinks aren't allowed in a lot of public places, like libraries, museums, and stores. That's because sticky foods and beverages tend to get spilled and ruin things. Most big places have snack bars or special areas for eating, so head for one of those, or head outside if your stomach starts growling.

Be willing to help the staff by cleaning up the area after you mess up. Good manners teach us to be good helpers.

That's Entertainment!

At a movie, play, or concert, it's important to be quiet so that the people around you can hear what's going on—and so you can follow along too! Clap or laugh when it's appropriate. (Watch for cues from other people.) Don't stand up and block the view of those behind you or whisper to your friend all through the show.

Cell phones should be turned off when you go to such events. If you need to call someone, excuse yourself and go out to the lobby to talk.

If you are eating snacks in the theater, remember that munching sounds carry a long way. Chew your food quietly.

Places of Worship

You've been invited to spend the night at Bevan's and go to church with him. The people at your church are very quiet throughout your service, standing only during certain prayers or songs and wearing nice suits and dresses. But at Bevan's church lots of people wear blue jeans and sneakers and sing and clap loudly. There's even a band with electric guitars and drums! It's like nothing you've experienced before. What do you do?

Keep in mind that Bevan would probably feel weird visiting your church too. You don't have to do anything that makes you feel uncomfortable. You can just close your eyes or stay seated. Be kind to anyone you meet and *don't* say, "Man, Bevan, your church is totally wacko!" It's better to say something like, "That was interesting, Bevan. It's fun to wear jeans to church."

Be very respectful when you are in church. You come there to worship God and to learn something about the Bible. Consider the others around you.

When Strangers Approach

You're at Disneyland when a total stranger starts chatting with you and asking you questions. Should you talk to him? How you respond depends on who you're with and what the person seems like. If you're alone, you need to be very careful. It's always good to be polite, of course, but you should also be smart. You can say,

"It's two o'clock," or "The hippopotamus display is over there." But don't tell him your name, where you live, or any other personal information. Walk away and find an adult you know or a park employee and tell him what happened. By the way, the same rules apply in another *huge* public place—the Internet. It's fun to check out Web sites and chat rooms, but remember that people on the Internet often aren't who they say they are. So keep any personal information *off* the Web.

Kid-2-Kid

At Ease in All Situations

Can you think of a place where you don't feel comfortable? We all can! Some places or situations where many kids your age feel uneasy are weddings, funerals, hospitals, rest homes, gatherings that are mainly for adults, religious ceremonies, graduations, and other formal events. Often guys will try to feel more relaxed in these places by laughing loudly, cracking jokes, or goofing around with a friend. Sometimes it's hard *not* to do these things, but you really need to use your best manners. Don't panic, though, if you goof up or say the wrong thing.

A Hearty Handshake

If you'll be doing a lot of shaking hands, you'll want to have a nice, hearty handshake. Here's how it's done. First, hold your hand out with your fingers together and your thumb up. Don't make a face if the other person squeezes too hard. And don't *you* squeeze too hard. Don't let your hand go limp. No one wants to shake hands with a jellyfish! Don't high-five or do fancy hand-shakes unless you know the other person likes to do that, and don't do silly handshakes in a serious place. If you meet a girl, you should wait for her to offer to shake hands first.

In the old days, girls did not shake hands, but in today's social scene they may extend a hand if they wish. It's okay for a young lady to shake hands if she wishes; just make sure that it is firm and accepting when you do.

Coming and Going

Sometimes it's hard to know what to say when you meet someone—and it's just as hard to figure out what to say when it's time to go! It's always nice to stand when you say hello, especially if you're meeting somebody older than you. Then smile, look at the person, shake hands, and say something like, "Hello," or "How are you today?" That's easy enough, isn't it? When it's time to say goodbye, there's not really any need to hang around. All you need to say is, "Bye, Chad," or "See you, Weston," or "Thanks for having me over, Aunt Donna. I always have fun at your house."

A courteous handshake or a warm hug is appropriate if you know the individual.

Out of the Spotlight

At an event like a wedding or graduation party, all of the attention is on just one or two people. It's their day to shine, so it's really rude if you try to turn the spotlight on yourself. To show respect to the person being honored, lend a hand when you can. Help your cousin and his new bride carry their luggage to the car. Show your relatives where to put their coats at your sister's graduation party. If you meet someone else who seems like he doesn't feel comfortable either, you can try talking to him.

Tongue-Tied

What should you do when you're feeling shy or when the right words just won't come out? If you're meeting someone new and no one introduces that person to you, just go ahead and introduce yourself. That's kind of hard sometimes. You might keep waiting for the other person to say hello. But go ahead and take the first step. You'll be glad you did. When you're talking to people you don't know very well, sometimes it's hard to know what to talk about after the hellos are finished. The very best way to handle this is to remember that everybody likes to talk about themselves. So just ask questions and listen to the answers in a friendly way.

Questions, Questions!

Okay, so now you know that asking questions is a good way to get the conversation going. But is it all right to ask any kind of question? Frankly, some questions are better to ask than others. Anything that has to do with how much something costs, how much someone weighs, or anything that seems really personal is not fair question material. For instance, don't ask Grandma, "Why did that police officer pull Grandpa over? Is he a bad driver?" You can, however, ask Uncle Bucky what it's like to be a farmer or cousin Sally how her ten cats are doing.

The Polite Truth

You've always been taught to tell the truth, right? But what do you do when someone asks you a question and the truth doesn't sound so hot? For instance, your friend Nick is in the hospital and he doesn't look well at all. When Nick's mom says, "Doesn't Nicky look wonderful?" you might be tempted to lie or to respond, "No, he looks terrible!" However, you know you shouldn't lie *or* make Nick feel bad. So just give your friend a big smile and say, "I'm so glad I could see you this week. I like that new hat. It looks like you're enjoying the book I loaned you." There are certain kinds of things that are better *not* to say. This is called being tactful, and it simply means that you don't say everything you're thinking, especially if what you're thinking might hurt someone's feelings.

▶ Kid-2-Kid ◀

Do We, or Don't We?

We all need a little help knowing how to handle some minor social annoyances. Do we, or don't we? That is the question. Guests just show up, and we aren't sure how to handle them. Here are a few tips:

To hug or not to hug. If the person is a close friend or relative, it's perfectly okay to give him a hug. Remember not to squeeze the air out of his body, particularly if you're bigger than he is. However, if you are being introduced for the first time, hold off on the hug but extend a hand for a shake and a "Hello, I'm glad to meet you!"

Sorry, what's your name? You may be unable to recall a person's name (that's why I like name tags). It's quite proper to say, "I'm sorry, I've forgotten your name; can you remind me, please." Don't try to fake it—that will just make things worse. On occasion, someone might call you by the wrong name. If it bothers you, you can very politely give him your correct name. If it doesn't bother you, just carry on and ignore the error.

Let's play soccer together. Don't say it if you don't mean it. Sometimes you might be tempted to say something just to be nice. If you don't mean it, don't suggest it. If you do mean it, be sure to follow up in a few days to make a plan to play together.

Watch your language. Be careful with your words. Don't be disrespectful to those in your presence by using improper language. Off-color jokes and the use of four-letter words are never appropriate. Be very respectful at all times. This also is a sign of self-respect.

Being late. This is a bad habit that seems difficult for some people to get a handle on. Tardiness shows disrespect for the people waiting. You don't want to get a reputation of being late. It's rude to call someone right when you're supposed to meet her to say you'll be late. Sometimes you can't help being late, and that can be okay, once in a while—emergencies do occur. Just don't make it a habit.

Yelling, whispering, and gossiping. What would a ball game be without yelling? Or a good movie without whispering to a friend? But gossiping is never appropriate. Your friends will trust and respect you when they know you can keep a secret they've shared with you. Good friends don't gossip about each other. Protect your own reputation by protecting that of others.

No nail clipping in public. Even though you may be bored or have time to kill, don't clip your fingernails or toenails in public, and don't polish them either. If these areas need maintenance, either visit a nail salon or take care of them at home, but never in public. A big manners error is to polish your nails in a confined space like a small room or an airplane. The fumes can give those near you headaches, and taking care of personal hygiene in public places is never appropriate.

Control the volume of your music. If you enjoy listening to music at home or at the beach, remember to keep the volume at a personal listening level. The person next to you may not like your choice of music (I know that's hard to believe). Making others feel good makes you feel good!

Chewing gum. Nothing is refreshing like a fresh stick of gum. It curbs your appetite, softens a dry mouth, and gives you something to do when you're bored. However, some rules apply when you decide to stick that gum in your mouth. If you are with others, make sure you offer them a stick too. When in public, please don't smack your jaws, blow bubbles, or snap your gum while chewing. And observe all gum-free zones and scenarios, including church, a baby dedication, or a museum.

Exchanging gifts with friends. Gift giving is not a contest of who can give the most expensive gift. You're only able to give what you can give. Your friendship is not based on money, so don't be in competition when it comes to gift giving.

Maybe some of these are obvious, but it is always helpful to have a friendly reminder to keep your public behavior pleasant and to treat others with respect and kindness.

> *So you've got a problem? That's good! Why?*
> *Because repeated victories over your problems are the*
> *rungs on your ladder to success. With each victory*
> *you grow in wisdom, stature and experience.*
> *You become a bigger, better, more successful person*
> *each time you meet a problem and tackle and*
> *conquer it with a positive mental attitude.*
>
> CLEMENT STONE

The Gift of Friendships and Relationships

Passing On Your Values

The best index to a person's character is (A) how he treats people who can't do him any good, and (B) how he treats people who can't fight back.

ABIGAIL VAN BUREN

One of the great joys of having children is passing on to a new generation values we feel are useful and necessary for a good life. We're not here on earth just to have fun and be friends with our offspring. As parents, we are to be teachers to our children. Being a parent includes a lot of responsibilities. It isn't easy.

The values you teach and model will become the foundation for how your child interacts with others and builds healthy relationships. If you've never done this before, take time to define and clarify your values. Below is a list of values to consider:

- religious beliefs
- family importance
- good manners (you've already proven this priority!)
- honorable behavior with good character

- generosity
- respect for ethnic and cultural differences
- self-discipline
- work ethic
- service to the community
- honesty and integrity
- loyalty and reliability
- good sportsmanship
- good financial skills
- value of marriage
- respect for authority
- an understanding of right and wrong

Once you've made your list, take the time to rank the values in importance. Share your values with your children through the lens of the Golden Rule so that your kids will have a heart for others.

This section explores how manners in motion lead to strong friendships and relationships. We'll touch on how boys and girls are to treat one another in friendship and when dating becomes a part of the picture. If your family is too young for the discussion of proper dating practices, this is still an opportunity to emphasize the foundation of friendship and respect that all solid relationships are built upon.

Model the Relational Manners

Practicing good manners in our everyday life is very important. Our children will learn by watching what we do. These are some of the ways we can mentor our children:

- Show empathy. Empathy is the capacity to understand how others feel, to walk in their shoes. We should encourage and praise our children when we see them showing empathy for another person or a pet. If empathy isn't encouraged, it may wither away. To develop this part of a child's behavior, take time to discuss feelings with your child. At a very young age, a child can identify emotional feelings such as these: happy, glad, angry, bored, sad, scared, and so on.

- Encourage your child to see how people of different backgrounds act, speak, and live. People from different cultures, religions, and value systems may respond differently than we do. Take time to talk about these differences.

- Praise your children when they are considerate to others. Continually be on the lookout for opportunities to praise children for good behavior. Positive reinforcement will encourage your children to repeat the good behavior without being told or asked to do so.

- Be concerned about others. Since you're the pacesetter in your children's lives, they will be influenced by what they see you doing. If you're empathetic to others, they'll also follow your lead. If you find a lost wallet on the sidewalk and attempt to locate the owner so you can return it, you'll have an opportunity to discuss the right thing to do in such a situation. Your children can learn many lessons of character development when they see you behaving in the right way.

- Practice what you preach. Children will see through you if your walk is different from your talk. Those little eyes have wide-angle lenses. They are watching so carefully to see how you respond to various conflicts that arise in your family's life. How do you respond to the policeman when he gives you a ticket for speeding? Are you able to forgive those who offend you? Can you control the tone of your voice when you are angry or stressed?

Your children will view others and make decisions about how to treat them by observing what you do when you encounter friends, family, neighbors, strangers, other parents, and other children. To be able to teach compassion to a new generation is one of the greatest gifts of parenting. Treasure it and share it!

Manners School Family Activity: Friend and Family Quiz

Even when you live with people, you don't always get to know their favorite and least favorite things. Sometimes the smallest details go unnoticed. It's great fun and very helpful to take the time to get to know one another. The depth and strength of a relationship comes as we learn about the person in good times and in bad and as we discover how to best be a friend.

The following game is one you can suggest your kids play with their friends so they can become better acquainted. Introduce the game to your children by first playing with your family members. They'll see how enjoyable it is and then will know how the game works.

It's easy! All you have to do is copy the questions below onto little slips of paper. (You can make up more questions if you want to.) Then fold each question in half and place in a wide-mouthed jar or a hat. Then you're ready to play.

You need at least three people for this "game show"—a "host" and at least two "contestants." The host draws a question and reads it out loud. The contestants write down their answers. Then each contestant tries to guess what the *other* person's answer was. Every right guess earns a point. After ten questions, add up the points and see who knows the other family members better. Now try another set of contestants, or let the host try. The person with the most points wins.

> What is your favorite color?
>
> If you could have any kind of pet, what would it be?
>
> If you could be any animal you like, what would you be?
>
> Name a food you really hate.
>
> What's your favorite singer or music group? What's your favorite song?
>
> Name a TV show you can't stand! What's your favorite TV show?
>
> What's your least favorite chore to do at home?
>
> What's your favorite flavor of ice cream?
>
> If you could travel anywhere in the world today, where would you go first?
>
> What's your favorite board game?
>
> What's your favorite sport to watch or play?
>
> If you could have your favorite birthday dinner, what would the main dish be?
>
> In what state or country were you born?
>
> Who is your favorite teacher?

If you could choose your own name, what would it be?

Name your favorite TV or movie star.

What's the best book you ever read?

How many people live at your house?

How many animals live at your house?

What is your favorite subject in school?

What is your least favorite subject?

Pull any questions that aren't relevant to your situation, and feel free to add some questions. Make it a fun family night.

Kid-2-Kid

How to Be a Friend

Everybody wants friends. Everybody needs friends. But have you ever stopped to wonder why?

You need friends to play games with. Some kinds of fun just aren't as much fun alone!

You need friends to talk to. Friends listen to your secrets and talk with you about your problems and all the good things that happen too. Sometimes you just need to talk for the fun of it!

You also need friends to learn from. My friends have shown me how to do all sorts of things—like roller-skate and make silhouette portraits. You need friends to give you ideas and to help you see things right. If I'm really confused about a problem, talking to a friend usually helps me sort it all out.

Sometimes you need friends to help you do things. Once

Elizabeth's room got so messy, she didn't even know where to start cleaning. But friends all came over to help, and we had that room clean in a couple of hours!

When you have good times, you need friends to help you enjoy them. When bad things happen, you need friends even more. Friends can help you feel a little happier when you're sad and a little braver when you're afraid. You need friends to make fun things more fun and not-so-much-fun things a little easier. And you need friends so you won't be lonely.

What Is a Friend?

A friend is a person who really cares about you—the *inside* you, not just your clothes or your stuff or your other friends.

1. Friends can trust each other.
2. Friends help each other.
3. Friends do things together.
4. Friends are loyal to each other.
5. Friends are honest with each other.
6. Friends are people you can talk to and who listen to you.
7. Friends share with each other.
8. Friends are there in the good times and the bad times.
9. Friends never judge you. They accept you for who you are.
10. Friends have fun together.

A friend is someone who will tell you the truth when you need to know it...but a friend is also someone who cares about your feelings and tries to understand you.

A friend is someone who likes the things you like, at least part of the time. A friend is somebody you enjoy being with.

And a friend is someone you can trust. A friend won't break promises or tell your secrets. A friend shows respect for you and doesn't try to get you in trouble.

My Grammie always says you should choose your friends carefully. I think that means you should make sure that everyone you call your friend really *is* your friend! It doesn't mean that someone has to be perfect to be your friend. Nobody's perfect. But if someone wants to be your friend, she should act like a friend.

And, of course, that goes for you too.

Alike and Different

Friends don't always have to be just like you.

They can be older or younger. They can even be relatives. My Aunt Jenny is my friend, even though she's my mother's sister. When I go over to her house, we can talk about *anything.*

Boys can be friends too. Chad, who lives next door to Aleesha, has been her friend for a long time. They like to play basketball in Chad's driveway. And sometimes Chad and Aleesha just sit outside on the steps and talk.

Friends can come in any color, and they can be from almost anywhere. Jasmine, our new friend, was born in China and was adopted by her mom in the United States. Maria's grandparents came from Mexico. Aleesha's family is African American, and my mom's family is Jewish. Elizabeth moved here from Texas, and Christine has always lived right here in this very town, in the same house where she lives now.

My friends are all a little different from one another. We like being different. Friends who are different from you can teach you interesting things. Different friends help you think of things you hadn't thought of before. They can help you be more understanding...and that can make the whole world a better place.

But just because we're different, that doesn't mean we're *completely* different. It would be hard to be friends if we didn't have anything in common.

Forever Friends

All friends are special, but some friends are *really* special.

These are the friends you know really, really well and like a whole lot. You think alike. You understand each other. You can't imagine ever not being friends. Some people call these special friends "best friends." But I like to call my special, special friends my "forever friends."

Christine and I are like that. We've been friends a long time and can't imagine not being close to each other. We've even talked about going to the same college someday!

That doesn't mean we have to do everything together. We don't!

And it doesn't mean we can't have *other* special friends. We do! Christine's really good friends with Maria, and I've started being good friends with Jasmine.

But when I have really big news to tell, or when Christine is really sad about something, or when one of us has a fantastic idea, guess who we call first? That's right. We reach for the phone and call our very special forever friend!

Finding a Forever Friend

But what if you don't have a special friend like that? Don't feel bad! Maybe you just haven't found your forever friend yet!

My Grammie says that special friends like Christine are a gift from God, and sometimes you just have to wait for them to come along. You can't *make* someone be a forever friend. You just have to wait and see.

But while you wait, there are lots of other things you can do. You can practice being a good, friendly person. And you can enjoy the friends you do have—because most forever friends start out as just ordinary, everyday friends. Then you get to know each other, and you share a lot of fun and maybe some tears, and one day you realize your friendship is really something special.

Appreciating Your Friends

Every so often I think you should look at all your friends—especially your forever friends—and think about what you like about them and then tell them. Every so often it's good to say, "I think you're special because..."

Sometimes it's hard to say something like that out loud. But you can say it in a card or a note. You can say it in a little tag that goes with a present you made yourself. You could put it in a song or poem and read it on an audio or video tape.

Of course, you can also say it by the way you treat your friends. When you listen to your friends, when you encourage them, when you do things their way (at least sometimes), you're really telling them, "I'm glad you're my friend."

When you remember to appreciate your friends, it makes you a better friend. And guess what? Trying to be a good friend is even more important than trying to *find* a good friend.

Even a forever friend!

Furry, Finny, and Feathery

Can an animal be your friend? My friends and I think so. My kitten, Angel, is a great listener, and I never feel lonely when she's purring in my lap. Christine's dog, Micky, is a good friend to all of us, and we also like Maria's hamsters, Aleesha's fish, Elizabeth's bunny, and Jasmine's cockatoo. All my friends think of their pets as their friends—but of course we like having people friends too!

▶ Kid-2-Kid ◀

For the Guys: How to Treat Girls

Okay, guys, you knew this one was coming—how to treat girls! "Do I really have to have good manners around girls?" you might be asking. "It's more fun to gross them out!" But this isn't just about how to act around girls your own age (although it is important to use good manners with them). This is also about the other "girls" you see every day (who are actually called "women")—your mom, your favorite aunt, your grammy, your teacher, your mom's best friend. You also might have some girls as buddies, and while good manners doesn't mean always letting Lexie win in H-O-R-S-E (especially because she usually wins anyway!), it's important to treat girls kindly, as you would treat any good friend.

Opening Doors

It might seem totally old-fashioned, but it is nice to open a door for a girl. Your mom will be so pleased when you do this for her!

It's also good manners to open doors for girls your own age. Some girls might not like it, though, and that's okay. You can take turns. In fact, it's good manners to open doors for *anyone*—including your big brother! And while we're on the subject of doors, be sure to always close them quietly. Slamming doors bothers everyone, especially if they slam shut in someone's face.

You Can Go First

It's also nice to give girls the first choice of something—the place before you in line, the last piece of pumpkin pie, even the first shot in that game of H-O-R-S-E. If she declines and lets you be first, go ahead. But it's still nice to offer. As boys, it always pays big when we are nice to the girls in our lives—that means Mom, sisters, aunts, the girl next door. Remember, girls go first.

Chairs and Coats

Next time you go out for ice-cream sundaes with Grammy, try helping her with her coat and pulling out the chair for her to sit in. (Just make sure you don't confuse Grammy with your pal B.J. and jokingly pull out the chair from under her!) If you do it right, you're sure to get a look of surprise followed by a great big smile followed by the Mondo Sundae—that quadruple-scoop, extra-nuts-and-whipped-cream, double-hot-fudge concoction you've been eyeing on the menu for years.

Say What?

When you're talking to girls, go ahead and talk about the things that interest you (and probably also interest them)—sports, music, computers, books—but leave out the gross stuff. It might be interesting to you, but Grammy (and just about anyone else, for that matter!) doesn't want to hear about how you and Juan captured slugs and learned all about their slime. And you can bet that Aunt Jenny really doesn't want to know how far a spit wad can fly. Don't worry, there are plenty of things left to talk about. You can always talk about slugs and spit wads the next time you and Juan get together.

You Mean There's a Difference?

Yes, there *is* a difference between boys and girls (and men and women). While we all share tons in common, it's important to respect girls for who and what they are—*girls*. That said, it's also important that you don't judge girls *just because* they're different (and you shouldn't judge *anyone* because they're different!). Don't automatically assume that because your sister is a girl, she doesn't like to play hockey or can't beat you at a computer game or does nothing but talk on the phone. She'll be eager to prove you wrong! Everyone is his or her own person, and the sooner you learn that, the more you can enjoy people for who they are—*themselves!*

Girls Are Great Friends

Did you know that it's fine to have girls as friends? Lots of guys your age do. But what do you do if your friends tease you about hanging out with a girl? The best thing to do is just shrug it off. Don't feel you have to slug or be rough with the girl who's your pal simply to prove that you don't "like" her. Instead, enjoy these friendships! Emmy is a fast runner, and she's fun to train with. (In fact, both of you have your eye on winning blue ribbons on Field Day!) Amy is an awesome soccer goalie. Anne knows a lot about nature and the outdoors. And Christine is a good baker.

You two love to make (and eat!) chocolate-chip cookies. Life would be boring if we only had one type of friend. So be proud of these friendships. Anyone who teases you probably wishes he had more people to hang out with.

Kid-2-Kid

For the Girls: How to Talk to Boys

I know that most girls aren't interested in boys until they are teenagers, but we all have boys in our lives. We have brothers, cousins, uncles, dads—boys are all over the place. The sooner you know how to talk with them, the more socially well rounded you will be. Yes, it's very ladylike to have good manners around your friends who are boys.

Boys Are Different

You probably already realize that boys are different from girls. They wear different clothes, play different games, make different sounds, like to get dirty. There is an old saying, "Boys are made of snips and snails and puppy-dogs' tails, and girls are made of sugar and spice and everything nice." As babies, boys wear blue and girls wear pink.

Just remember, you don't have to act like them, and they don't have to act like you. When around boys, be yourself.

Give Boys a Chance

Even though you are very capable of opening a door, be patient and let the young man open the door for you. This gives the boy a chance to be a polite gentleman. When you are both offered a platter of cookies, wait for him to let you choose yours first. Wait for him to let you go ahead of him when standing in line or when going through a door. Patience really pays big dividends when you will let a boy be a gentleman. Learn to wait!

What to Talk About

Quite often boys will talk about different subjects than girls do. Learn what your friends who are boys like to talk about. If baseball is their favorite sport, learn about baseball. Most boys like football, so have your dad or big brother tell you about football. Be interested in what they're interested in. Boys don't usually like drawn-out stories, so give them a shortened version of what happened. A lot of boys are shy, so you have to ask questions that require an answer other than "yes" or "no." When you are finished talking with a boy, very politely excuse yourself by saying, "It was so much fun talking with you. I hope we can talk again soon."

Telephone Manners

The ladylike manner is to wait until the boy calls you first. It is best not to call a boy first. It is his role to take the first step. When he does call, be aware that you have homework and chores; so limit how much time you spend on the phone. Be polite when you have to end the conversation, by saying, "It was good talking to you. I have a lot of homework for tomorrow." Proper manners would be the same for text messaging.

Boys Are Great Friends

It is good to have boys as friends. After all, there will always be boys in your life, so knowing how to be friends with them will come in handy. If you have brothers in your family, you are at an advantage because you know a little bit about how to act around boys. If there are no boys in your family other than Dad, it will take longer to figure boys out. If you need help, remember that Dad can give you good advice.

Older Kid-2-Older Kid

Oh No! Date Time

No matter what the ages of your children they eventually will think about dating. When that time comes you will want to review with them certain manners that go along with their age in life.

PaPa Bob always told the boys and grandboys to remember:

> Be a gentleman going in,
> Be a gentleman when you are in, and
> Be a gentleman when you leave.

This thought is etched in their minds. They are now in their early twenties and they seemed to live by this code in their dating experiences.

The standards for proper manners regarding dating and courtship have certainly changed over the past twenty years. However, good manners never go out of style, and a few guidelines can still help you as you start to date.

What Is a Date?

A date is between a young man and a young woman who plan

on getting together at a specified time to do something special. It's a date when someone asks you to go to a football game, a movie, to church, on a picnic, horseback riding, and the like.

A date could be a formal event or something as casual as going out for lunch or ice cream, going skateboarding, or playing volleyball on the beach.

It is still proper for the guy to ask directly or on the telephone for that first date. Girls, hold back, and let the guy take the leadership. Even though many girls today call to ask for and set a date, believe me—the guy would prefer to do the asking.

If you happen to be shy and aren't really sure about being alone with the other person, plan to double-date. This takes a lot of pressure off of you until you get to know the person a little bit better. It's also a safer way to initially get to know someone.

Dating Manners

- Give someone a call at least three days before you want to set a day and time.
- Make that first date one that is a match for the other person's interests: a movie if she likes a movie, a baseball game if she likes sports, or a walk on the beach or a trail hike if she is athletic.
- Try not to change plans at the last minute.
- Be on time.
- Dress for the occasion. After all, you want to make a good impression.
- Be sensitive to the other person's budget if you are choosing the activity and the other person is paying.
- Keep the conversation on upbeat topics.

- If you don't feel well or if you are tired, try to be positive in your attitude.

- At the end of the date, express a heartfelt thanks, even if the chemistry wasn't too positive between the two of you.

- Try to laugh and have a pleasant sense of humor.

- If the date is going in the wrong direction, you have the right to excuse yourself. If you grow uncomfortable with your date's behavior, take whatever steps are necessary to escape from the situation, whether that means calling your parents, asking the restaurant manager to help you, or calling 911 from your cell phone if the situation becomes really difficult. This probably won't happen, but if it does, act on it. Trust your instincts.

- If the person wants to see you again and you would like to have another date, you can certainly say yes. If, however, you weren't on the same wavelength and you don't want another date, you might as well nip it in the bud and say, "No, I don't think that would be a good idea." It's okay to be firm and frank. Be courteous but direct.

Love is very patient and kind...If you love someone you will always believe in him, always expect the best of him...Love goes on forever.

1 CORINTHIANS 13:4-7 (AUTHOR PARAPHRASE)

Happy Graduation!

Now that you and your children have gone through these many tips and ideas for making manners a part of your life, you can have a manners graduation party. The children will put all they've learned into this final test.

For a graduation exercise, choose an activity for your child or children so that they can showcase their best manners. Here are some ideas to get you thinking:

- Have the children prepare a meal and serve it to you, Mom and Dad.

- Choose a formal restaurant to go to as a family so everyone can show off their silverware savvy and their formal manners. (Be sure that the kids do their own ordering so that they practice politely speaking up in formal settings.)

- Have a casual neighborhood party. Make your kids the official hosts so they get to practice their hospitality

manners while planning the party and while the party
is happening.

- Host a formal adult gathering, and have the children
  be a part of the planning, the execution, and perhaps even the entertainment for the evening! If it's a
  tea party, they could help serve the tea as well as be
  in charge of playing the piano or reading poetry to
  the guests.

- Let your children choose a way to demonstrate their
  manners. Their ideas are frequently the best ones.

Plan to Praise

Praise the efforts of your children. They long to hear words of
encouragement and cheer from their parents and their siblings.
You reinforce the use of manners by noticing when your child
does something right. It becomes too easy to comment on the
negative behaviors or the slipups. Don't be a parent who misses
out on the wonders of celebrating the evidences of compassion
and kindness that your child expresses.

For this graduation, make a big deal out of their efforts and
growth. I encourage you to create certificates of achievement to
present at the graduation activity. Personalize the certificates to
reference a child's specific area of growth if you can.

❧

And may I take this final moment with you to praise your
efforts to make learning manners a priority for your family. Your
child's future friends, coworkers, spouse, and offspring will be
very appreciative of what you have accomplished by working

through the topics and exercises in this book. And your child will become an adult who understands that manners really are the beginning of kindness and confidence...and that they are a legacy worth passing along.

A child only educated at school is an uneducated child.

GEORGE SANTAYANA

Reference Materials

Emilie Barnes, *A Little Book of Manners: Courtesy & Kindness for Young Ladies* (Eugene, OR: Harvest House Publishers, 1998).

Emilie Barnes, *My Best Friends and Me: Fun Things to Do Together* (Eugene, OR: Harvest House Publishers, 1999).

Bob and Emilie Barnes, *A Little Book of Manners for Boys: A Game Plan for Getting Along with Others* (Eugene, OR: Harvest House Publishers, 2000).

Emilie Barnes, *Good Manners for Every Occasion: How to Look Smart and Act Right* (Eugene, OR: Harvest House Publishers, 2008).

More Great Books from Bob and Emilie Barnes

Good Manners for Every Occasion

While adults prompt young ones to practice their manners, many grown-ups are ready for a refresher course. Bestselling author Emilie Barnes is excited to share how manners strengthen adult relationships, professional interactions, social gatherings, and family ties as adults learn the art of introductions, communication, and sharing values with children.

A Little Hero in the Making
Illustrations by Michal Sparks

Fun lessons from Emilie encourage boys to develop the character and strength of a hero, and engaging illustrations by artist Michal Sparks inspire young ones to discover the super powers of manners.

A Little Princess in the Making
Illustrations by Michal Sparks

Emilie shares how little girls can become princesses by learning their manners. Gems of wisdom alongside paintings by artist Michal Sparks reveal how to be a kind and courteous young lady.

Simple Secrets Couples Should Know

Beloved authors Bob and Emilie Barnes have been married for more than 54 years and share their success in this book. Their insights and knowledge help couples develop and experience a thriving, God-centered marriage. Readers learn that good marriages don't just happen—they are carefully cultivated through deliberate choices.

The Quick-Fix Home Organizer

Home-management expert Emilie Barnes, whose books have sold more than 4.5 million copies, has a vast collection of home- and life-organization tips to share. This book is packed with brief, practical, and inspirational ideas to help readers create homes filled with peace and personality.

To contact Bob and Emilie Barnes to find out more about More Hours in My Day time-management and organization seminars or to buy More Hours in My Day products, please visit:

www.EmilieBarnes.com

or write to

More Hours in My Day
2150 Whitestone Dr.
Riverside, CA 92506

or call

951-682-4714

To learn more about books by Bob and Emilie Barnes
or to read sample chapters, log on to our website:

www.harvesthousepublishers.com

HARVEST HOUSE PUBLISHERS
EUGENE, OREGON